THE BEST
WNES
IN THE
S PER
MARKETS
2013

THE BEST W🍷NES IN THE S🍷PER MARKETS 2013

NED HALLEY

foulsham
LONDON • NEW YORK • TORONTO • SYDNEY

foulsham

Capital Point, 33 Bath Road, Slough, Berkshire
SL1 3UF, England

Foulsham books can be found in all good bookshops and direct
from www.foulsham.com

ISBN: 978-0-572-04000-0

Text copyright © 2013 Ned Halley
Series, format and layout design © W. Foulsham & Co. Ltd

Cover photographs © Thinkstock

A CIP record for this book is available from the British Library

The moral right of the author has been asserted

Printed and bound in Great Britain by Martins the Printers Ltd

Contents

It's really okay to drink
— supermarket wines —

The supermarkets are always in trouble for something. It's usually for squeezing independent retailers, including wine merchants, out of the market. Or it's for crushing the life out of suppliers by screwing prices down below the cost of production.

Occasionally, it's something a bit more particular. This year, besides the customary lobbyist hysteria about supermarkets selling cheap booze and precipitating everything from binge drinking to the demise of the British pub, it has been a very public complaint from a wine-trade grandee that supermarket wines are 'incredibly dull' and we shouldn't waste our money on them. Graham Mitchell, a member of the dynasty that owns the famed 130-year-old London merchant and wine-bar operator El Vino, says that much of the cheaper wine on sale in the UK 'lacks character, is bland and blended for the mass-market brands, and massively discounted in a supermarket or big retail chain'. Shoppers, he advises, should avoid £2.99 wines and invest at least £9.99: 'Although it's only three times the price, you are getting eight times the quality.'

I had to address these trenchant views when I was contacted by a reporter from *The Independent* newspaper. As the author of *The Best Wines in the Supermarkets*, would I like to comment on what Mr Mitchell had to say?

Well, I had to agree about £2.99 wines. The 2012 Budget raised the excise duty on still wine to £1.90 per 75cl, which puts the non-tax value of a £2.99 bottle at 60p. Yes, that's £2.39 duty and VAT, leaving just the 60p to cover the cost of making the wine, bottling and transporting it, and earning margins for the producer, the importer/distributor and the supermarket. It doesn't compute. Which explains why the £2.99 bottle of wine is (or should be) extinct.

Mr Mitchell's assertion that £9.99 is the threshold for good wine is much less clear-cut. The idea that one wine can be eight times better than another holds no water at all. Tasting great numbers of wines as I do, I have learned a universal principle: price is an unreliable guide to how much you can expect to like any individual wine.

The average retail price we pay in the supermarkets for wine is about £4.60 a bottle. That's less than half Mr Mitchell's minimum, but it is also half as much again as £2.99. It demonstrates that we are indeed willing to pay a sensible amount for wine, starting at somewhere around a fiver.

This year I have found close to 500 wines to recommend in this 2013 edition of *The Best Wines in the Supermarkets*, and one in five of them is priced at under £6. Sixty of these come in under £5, including 15 under £4, and none below £3. But the greatest number of wines, unsurprisingly, fall into the space between £6 and £10, taking the proportion of wines below Mr Mitchell's threshold to about three-quarters of the overall total.

But that's supermarket wines for you. The retail giants don't place a lot of emphasis on 'fine wines' –

if wines costing £10-plus can be defined as such. In fact, after doing this count of wines in the different price brackets, I find myself a little surprised that more than a hundred of those I have picked out do exceed £10. My own instinctive parsimony, amplified by the continuing economic crisis, makes me wary of extravagance. So anything I recommend above a tenner (and very occasionally above a twenty) is a serious recommendation indeed.

This is a suitable point at which to mention the scoring system I use in this book. It's a simple 0 to 10 scale, but it is strictly relative, because I take the price of each wine closely into consideration. At the time of tasting, I fix each wine at a point on the scale. When you're tasting 100 or even 200 wines in a single session, you have to score them in situ. There's no chance of recalling how much you liked more than a handful of individual wines from a really long day. Any wines I have noted with a score of 6 or above get keyed into the longlist from which the final selection is drawn. Only a few of the 6- or 7-scoring wines make the cut, because while I liked them, I might have been unconvinced on value grounds. It is the 8-scoring wines that make up the greatest number. They are absolutely sound wines at what I believe to be justifiable prices. A score of 9 indicates special interest and value. A score of 10 goes to any wine I have found exceptionally delicious, at a completely fair price.

All that said, I must muddy the waters again by mentioning discounts. Supermarkets are addicted to them. There are regular price wars. During this persistent recession, Sainsbury's and Tesco have frequently reduced wine prices by as much as 25 per cent for multiple purchases (usually six bottles) for a week or two at a time. Very often, these periods coincide exactly. I don't know who starts it. Asda goes in for similar promos known as 'roll-backs', and even Waitrose always has a long list of wines on discount, regularly of up to a third off the shelf price.

Online, Marks & Spencer is forever offering big cuts in case prices. This sometimes applies to the entire range. Tesco does the same. These offers are not necessarily extended to the stores, so bargain hunters should make a habit of checking the respective websites.

The most persistent discounter of them all is Majestic. At any one time, maybe half the wines are on multibuy offer: buy two bottles, get 20 per cent off. Given that the Majestic miracle has been manifested by the policy of a minimum purchase (now six bottles, any mix) it makes this choice of promotion method a no-brainer. It certainly seems to work. Majestic is booming, and the sole survivor among the national high street wine merchant chains. Much as I admire the wines – diversity and quality both run deep – I don't believe they'd have done it without the discounts.

In this edition, there has been a new entrant among the supermarkets and, I'm sad to say, an exit. Aldi, the no-frills chain, is the debutante. Although I have over the years occasionally popped into both Aldi and Lidl branches to buy a few aspirant-looking wines, I have not been able to summon up enough enthusiasm to make a listing among *The Best Wines in the Supermarkets*. But now Aldi has kindly let me taste a selection from its 'core' range – the wines you're most likely to find on shelf, as distinct from occasional special parcels – and I have liked a good number of them. Welcome aboard!

The exit is the Lancashire-based supermarket chain EH Booth. This redoubtable, family-owned company remains very much in business, and still has a range of about 800 wines on offer to shoppers in its 28 branches in northern England. But Booths has now closed its web-based operation, everywine.co.uk, which made a huge selection of wines available to online customers nationwide. I can therefore no longer include the company in the guide.

After the disappearance of Somerfield, and before that Safeway, it's a sorrow to say goodbye to another national supermarket wine retailer. But there is consolation. The quality of the wines in the burgeoning national chains (*pace* Mr Mitchell) continues to thrill. And many of the most exciting bottles are the ones bearing the retailer's own name. Naturally, the teams of buyers in the Big Four who acquire the wines for their own ranges – Asda's Extra Special, Morrisons' The Best, Sainsbury's Taste the Difference and Tesco's Finest – take particular pride in products for which they are closely responsible. The Masters of Wine and other experts now employed by all the big chains don't just choose the wines, they play a big part in making them.

There was a time when it was naff to serve a supermarket own-label wine at a dinner party. Now, maybe partly legitimised by the radical chic that rightly seeps into consumer behaviour during a prolonged recession, it's another story. I would venture to suggest it's really quite cool to put, say, a bottle of Sainsbury's Languedoc Blanc or Tesco Faugères on the table. These wines, both well under a tenner, are superb examples of their kind, and better value at today's prices than ever before. I have had no hesitation in giving each of them maximum points in this edition.

Look at it this way. Any mug with a fistful of money can buy decent wine. Choosing a good bottle on a tight budget takes discrimination, enthusiasm, knowledge and an eye for a bargain. That's what buying wine from a supermarket is all about. And it's fun.

Take my word for it. It's really OK to drink supermarket wines.

Age and strength

A word on alcohol levels and vintages. In the listings, I mention the alcohol by volume in the wine where it is either below 12 per cent or 14 per cent upwards. For readers to whom this information is significant, I hope this is of some help.

Nearly all the wines in the listings are made entirely or substantially from the harvest of the year stated on the label. If no vintage date is given, the wine will have been blended from harvests of two or more years. This is routine for some cheaper wine, and need not matter much, except with dry whites which, on principle, are the better for being newer and fresher. An undated dry white is best consumed at the first opportunity, if at all.

——A sense of place——

This book categorises the wines by nation of origin. It is largely to follow the manner in which retailers arrange their wines, but also because it is the country or region of origin that still most distinguishes one style of wine from another. True, wines are now commonly labelled most prominently with their constituent grape variety, but to classify all the world's wines into the small number of principal grape varieties would make for categories of an unwieldy size.

Chardonnay, Sauvignon Blanc and Pinot Grigio are overwhelmingly dominant among whites, and four grapes – Cabernet Sauvignon, Grenache, Merlot and Syrah (also called Shiraz) – account for a high proportion of red wines made worldwide.

But each area of production still – in spite of creeping globalisation – puts its own mark on its wines. Chardonnays from France remain (for the moment at least) quite distinct from those of Australia. Cabernet Sauvignon grown in a cool climate such as that of Bordeaux is a very different wine from Cabernet cultivated in the cauldron of the Barossa.

Of course there are 'styles' that winemakers worldwide seek to follow. Yellow, oaky Chardonnays of the type pioneered in South Australia are now made in South Africa, too – and in new, high-tech wineries in New Zealand and Chile, Spain and Italy. But the variety is still wide. Even though the 'upfront' high-alcohol wines of the New World have grabbed so much of the market, France continues to make the elegant wines it has always made in its classic regions. Germany still produces racy, delicate Rieslings, and the distinctive zones of Italy, Portugal and Spain make ever more characterful wines from indigenous grapes, as opposed to imported global varieties.

Among less expensive wines, the theme is, admittedly, very much a varietal one. The main selling point for most 'everyday' wines is the grape of origin rather than the country of origin. It makes sense, because the characteristics of various grape varieties do a great deal to identify taste. A bottle of white wine labelled 'Chardonnay' can reasonably be counted on to deliver that distinctive peachy or pineappley smell and soft, unctuous apple flavours. A Sauvignon Blanc should evoke gooseberries, green fruit and grassy freshness. And so on.

For all the domination of Chardonnay and Cabernet, there are plenty of other grape varieties making their presence felt. Argentina, for example, has revived the fortunes of several French and Italian varieties that had become near-extinct at home. And the grape that (in my view) can make the most exciting of white wines, the Riesling, is now doing great things in the southern hemisphere as well as at home in Germany.

Among the current market trends, the rise of rosé continues apace. Now accounting for one out of every eight bottles of still wine sold, the choice of pink brands has simply exploded. I have certainly found a greater number of interesting pinks than might have been imagined a few years ago, but there are still plenty of dull ones with suspiciously high levels of residual sugar, so choose carefully.

Rosé wines are supposed to be made from black-skinned grapes. After the crush, the skins are left in contact with the juice for long enough to impart a pleasing colour, and maybe some flavour with it, and the liquids and solids are then separated before the winemaking process continues as it would for white wine.

Some rosés are made merely by blending red and white wines together. Oddly enough, this is how all (bar one or two) pink champagnes are made, as permitted under the local appellation rules. But under prevailing regulations in Europe, the practice is otherwise forbidden. Elsewhere in the world, where winemaking is very much less strictly standardised, blending is no doubt common enough.

It is, I know, a perpetual source of anguish to winemakers in tightly regulated European nations that they have to compete in important markets like Britain with producers in Australia, the Americas and South Africa who can make and label their wines just as they please. Vineyard irrigation, the use of oak chips, and the blending in of wines from other continents are all permitted in the New World and eschewed in the Old.

But would we have it any other way? No winemaker I have met in Bordeaux or Barolo, Bernkastel or Rias Baixas seriously wants to abandon the methods and conventions that make their products unique – even with an eye on creating a global brand. And in this present difficult economic climate for wine drinkers (and winemakers) worldwide, this assurance of enduring diversity is a comfort indeed.

Spot the grape

The character of most wines is defined largely by the grape variety, and it is a source of innocent pleasure to be able to identify which variety it is without peeking at the label. Here are some of the characteristics to look for in wines from the most widely planted varieties.

White

Chardonnay: Colour from pale to straw gold. Aroma can evoke peach, pineapple, sweet apple. Flavours of sweet apple, with creaminess or toffee from oak contact.

Fiano: Italian variety said to have been cultivated from ancient Roman times in the Campania region of southern Italy. Now widely planted on the mainland and in Sicily, it makes dry but soft wines of colours ranging from pale to pure gold with aromas of honey, orchard fruit, almonds and candied apricot. Well-made examples have beautifully balanced nutty-fresh flavours. Fiano is becoming fashionable.

Pinot Grigio: In its home territory of north-east Italy, it makes wines of pale colour, and pale flavour too. What makes the wine so popular might well be its natural low acidity. Better wines are more aromatic, even smoky, and pleasingly weighty in the manner of the Pinot Gris made in Alsace – now being convincingly imitated in both Argentina and New Zealand.

Riesling: In German wines, pale colour, sharp-apple aroma, racy fruit whether dry or sweet. Faint spritz common in young wines. Petrolly hint in older wines. Australian and New Zealand Rieslings have more colour and weight, and often a minerally, limey twang.

Sauvignon Blanc: In the dry wines, pale colour with suggestions of green. Aromas of asparagus, gooseberries, nettles, seagrass. Green, grassy fruit.

Semillon: Colour can be rich yellow. Aromas of tropical fruit including pineapple and banana. Even in dry wines, hints of honey amid fresh, fruit-salad flavours.

Viognier: Intense pale-gold colour. Aroma evokes apricots, blanched almonds and fruit blossom. Flavours include candied fruits. Finish often low in acidity.

Red

Cabernet Sauvignon: Dense colour, purple in youth. Strong aroma of blackcurrants and cedar wood ('cigar box'). Flavour concentrated, often edged with tannin so it grips the mouth.

Grenache: Best known in the Côtes du Rhône, it tends to make red wines pale in colour but forceful in flavour with a wild, hedgerow-fruit style and hints of pepper.

Merlot: Dark, rich colour. Aroma of sweet black cherry. Plummy, rich, mellow fruit can be akin to Cabernet but with less tannin. May be hints of bitter chocolate.

Pinot Noir: Colour distinctly pale, browning with age. Aromas of strawberry and raspberry. Light-bodied wine with soft-fruit flavours but dry, clean finish.

Sangiovese: The grape of Chianti and now of several other Italian regions, too. Colour is fine ruby, and may be relatively light; a plummy or even pruny smell is typical, and flavours can evoke blackcurrant, raspberry and nectarine. Tannin lingers, so the wine will have a dry, nutskin-like finish.

Shiraz or Syrah: Intense, near-black colour. Aroma of ripe fruit, sometimes spicy. Robust, rich flavours, commonly with high alcohol, but with soft tannins. The Shiraz of Australia is typically much more substantial than the Syrah of the south of France.

Tempranillo: Colour can be pale, as in Rioja. Blackcurrant aroma, often accompanied by vanilla from oak ageing. Tobacco, even leather, evoked in flavours.

There is more about all these varieties, and many others, in 'What wine words mean' starting on page 123.

Looking for a branded wine?

While the supermarkets' own-label wines – the likes of the Sainsbury's Taste the Difference and the Tesco Finest ranges – are obviously exclusive to the respective chains, branded wines are very often stocked by any number of different retailers.

If you're looking for a favourite brand, do check the index to this book on page 186. If I have tasted the wine and given it a mention, it is most likely to appear under the heading of the supermarket that hosted the tasting. But you might be accustomed to seeing this particular wine in another chain altogether.

I cannot give space in a pocket-sized book to repetitions of notes on popular brands that might very well be sold by each of the supermarket chains. But I do try to keep tasting the bestselling brands in hope of finding something positive to say about them.

The outstanding buys:
—Europe is well on top—

The best wines in the supermarkets, it seems, are French. Although I taste and take notes on the wines for each edition of this guide over a period of several months, I extract a list of the top-scoring wines only at the very end of the process. This year, out of 32 wines I have garlanded with 10 points out of 10, I am astonished to discover that 16 are from France.

It goes against the grain. If I am asked to which country I would turn for wine supplies if my choice was limited to one only, I invariably answer Italy. But this year, I find, I have awarded only four perfect scores to Italian wines, equal in second place with Spain. New Zealand comes fourth with two, and Australia, England, Portugal, Romania, South Africa and the United States follow on with one apiece. Overall, it marks a somewhat stark global imbalance: Old World 27; New World 5.

Distribution of the honours among the retailers turns out to be rather more even. Sainsbury's comes first this year with eight top-scoring wines – six of them own-labels – followed by Tesco with six (four of them own-labels). Asda, Majestic, Marks & Spencer and Waitrose tie with four apiece for third place, while Aldi and Morrisons both have one.

My top wines of the year

Red wines

House Pinot Noir	Sainsbury's	£4.49
Finest Côtes Catalanes Grenache 2010	Tesco	£7.79
Extra Special Chianti Classico Riserva 2008	Asda	£7.98
Taste the Difference Faugères 2010	Sainsbury's	£7.99
Juliénas Duboeuf 2010	Tesco	£8.99
Finest Viña Mara Rioja Reserva 2007	Tesco	£9.49
Noster Nobilis 2007	Asda	£9.98
Home Ranch Pinot Noir 2009	M&S	£9.99
Squinzano Monte Nobile Rosso Riserva 2008	Tesco	£9.99
Extra Special New Zealand Pinot Noir 2009	Asda	£10.18
Héritage de Pierre Lurton 2009	M&S	£10.99
Gulf Station Pinot Noir 2010	Sainsbury's	£11.99
The Ned Pinot Noir 2010	Majestic	£12.49
Quinta da Bacalhôa 2008	Majestic	£13.49
Taste the Difference Châteauneuf du Pape 2010	Sainsbury's	£14.99
Viña Ardanza Rioja Reserva Especial 2001	Majestic	£22.00
Torre de Mastio Amarone della Valpolicella Classico 2008	Sainsbury's	£22.99

White wines

Asda Marsanne 2011	Asda	£4.47
Falanghina Beneventano 2011	M&S	£5.99
Finest Swartland Chenin Blanc 2011	Tesco	£6.99
Finest Picpoul de Pinet 2011	Tesco	£7.29
Fief Guérin Muscadet Côtes de Grandlieu Sur Lie 2011	Waitrose	£7.49
Domaine de Vieux Vauvert 2011	Waitrose	£8.99
Taste the Difference Languedoc Blanc 2011	Sainsbury's	£8.99
Caixas Albariño Rias Baixas 2011	Majestic	£9.99
Morrisons The Best Chablis 2009	Morrisons	£10.19
Taste the Difference Pouilly Fumé 2010	Sainsbury's	£12.79
Arnaud de Villeneuve Ambré Hors d'Age Rivesaltes 1985	Waitrose	£13.99
Joseph Drouhin Rully Premier Cru 2010	Waitrose	£14.99

Sparkling wines

Philippe Michel Crémant de Jura	Aldi	£6.99
Sainsbury's Blanc de Noirs Champagne Brut	Sainsbury's	£20.99
English Sparkling Rosé	M&S	£22.00

 Until I actually tasted a reasonable cross-section of the wines on offer at no-frills supermarket Aldi, I had blithely assumed their principal attraction would be price. This turns out to be wrong. Some of the prices are indeed low, but not at the expense of quality.

I asked the company, which has 7,000 stores worldwide, 400 of them in Britain, if it has a philosophy as far as wine is concerned. Like other supermarket chains, Aldi likes to say how well it gets on with its suppliers.

'Aldi works with some of the world's leading wineries to deliver the very best products for our stores, both in the UK and abroad,' the spokesman told me. 'We enjoy close and often long-term working relationships with our suppliers – to whom we are able to guarantee the delivery of significant and consistent volumes of product. Due to the mutually beneficial nature of these partnerships, therefore, wineries are able to offer us some of the most competitive costs on the market.'

It makes sense. Aldi buys a vast quantity of wine, and therefore gets a good deal.

'Aldi also operates according to a simple and highly efficient business model, which allows for far tighter margins than most multiple retailers,' the spokesman added. 'So when a shopper buys a bottle of wine from

Aldi, they can be confident that the majority of their spend is going into the liquid itself.'

Well, yes, though in Britain the value of the liquid in a £3.49 wine such as Aldi's splendid Montepulciano d'Abruzzo cannot be said to account for the majority of the price (£2.52 of the price is tax), but I do see what they're trying to say. And some of the wines really are quite remarkably good for the money.

Last word to Aldi: 'We are justifiably proud of the quality of our wine range, particularly the numerous award-winning products within it, and, while we always strive to deliver everyday great value to our customers, we will never compromise on quality to achieve a price point.'

Red Wines

AUSTRALIA

7 Kooliburra Shiraz Cabernet 2011   £3.99
Unexpected cherry nose carries on into the fruit, where its sweetness is abruptly counteracted by a coaly dryness and grip of toasty tannin. It's perfectly wholesome and undeniably cheap.

6 Bushland Barossa Valley Shiraz 2011   £4.99
Jammy-smelling and surprisingly light in weight (though 14% alcohol) given its origin, but this does have fruit and balance.

CHILE

8 Tierra del Sol Cabernet Sauvignon 2011   £3.99
Properly made, wholesome middleweight Cabernet of character is firmly fruity and well-balanced; roasty backtaste is not unpleasant.

FRANCE

8 Côtes du Rhône 2011   £3.59
Strong purple colour and boiled-sweet nose; this young-tasting wine is spicily correct in style, and finishes neatly tight. Nice label.

6 Bordeaux Supérieur 2010   £4.99
Rather sweet and soft and bland middleweight Cabernet Merlot of uncertain Bordelais origin made by famed flying winemaker Jacques Lurton is inoffensive and could be from anywhere.

ITALY

8 Montepulciano d'Abruzzo 2010   £3.49
Brambly whiff of healthy hedgerow fruit comes off this well-coloured, bouncing, friendly pasta-matching red. I cannot understand how they do it at the price.

RED WINES

ITALY

7 **San Zenone Toscana Rosso 2009** £3.99
Sweetish blackcurrant style with cherry whiff and decent concentration in spite of light weight and colour.

SPAIN

8 **Toro Loco Tempranillo 2011** £3.59
Smartly packaged Utiel-Requena middleweight has sweet cassis centre and a clean, dry finish; respectable picnic or party red.

8 **Minarete Ribera del Duero 2010** £5.49
Dark and minty Tempranillo from a much-esteemed red-wine region has recognisable intense, slinky style with an unexpected teeth-coating background sweetness. Big wine for food with big flavours, including spicy dishes.

9 **Baron Amarillo Rioja Reserva 2006** £5.99
The name sounds contrived, but this is the genuine article, a middleweight, clean, authentically blackcurrant Rioja with well-judged oak, benefiting from maturity with no sign of senility. As good as it gets for this money.

WHITE WINES

CHILE

🍷 9 Tierra del Sol Sauvignon Blanc 2011 £3.99
Water white but terrifically crisp, fresh, light wine with grassy Sauvignon character and refreshing quality. I cannot fault it, especially at this price.

FRANCE

🍷 9 Bordeaux Blanc 2011 £4.19
Zippy, dry, Sauvignon-based wine is completely convincing: rush of gooseberry-grass flavour with a firmly limey acidity.

🍷 6 Mâcon Villages 2011 £4.99
Pineapple and spearmint on the nose of this recognisable but spongy Chardonnay.

N. ZEALAND

🍷 8 Freeman's Bay Sauvignon Blanc 2011 £4.99
Kiwi wines are scarce at under a fiver, and this brisk Sauvignon is respectable for the money, fresh and grassy.

SPARKLING WINES

FRANCE

🍷 **10** **Philippe Michel Crémant de Jura** £6.99

An Aldi stalwart for as long as I can remember, this bottle-fermented pure Chardonnay from the Jura, southeast of Burgundy, is creamily sparkling, toasty ripe, dry-finishing, and fresh as a daisy. Amazing value.

ITALY

🍷 **9** **Valdobbiadene Prosecco Superiore** £6.99

It looks good in its shapely bottle, and tastes pretty good too: a dry style with persistent mousse, fresh orchard fruit and well-judged citrus edge. Good value.

Asda

For the past five years at least, Asda wines have been getting better and better. I know this because I have tasted a wide range of the wines every year since 2008, and this year's tasting was the best ever.

The great highlight is the Extra Special range. They are the wines that Philippa Carr, the Master of Wine in charge at Asda, stakes her reputation on. They are hand-picked, and many are made with the assistance (or perhaps more than that) of Philippa and her colleagues.

Starting at about £6 a bottle, these wines are consistently of inspired quality, and run other supermarket premium wines very close indeed. The same is true of Asda's bargain wines, some well under £5. 'There are a lot of customers who enjoy wine but really cannot afford more than maybe £5 for a bottle,' Philippa has told me. 'Our job is to find good wines for this sort of price. It's what we do.'

AUSTRALIA

🍷 9 **De Bortoli Reserve Cabernet Sauvignon 2009**   £7.48
Intense, toasty-oaked Cabernet of huge character (and 14.5% alcohol) has fine weight and balance; it is spot on, and at the price a remarkable buy.

🍷 8 **Extra Special McLaren Vale Shiraz 2009**   £8.48
Nice soupy-spicy Barossa smoothie by Tatachilla; don't be deterred by the ghastly label.

CHILE

🍷 9 **Casillero del Diablo Cabernet Sauvignon 2011**   £7.33
Ubiquitous but entirely admirable Concha y Toro brand is such a dependable buy, with part new-oaked sweetly ripe fruit and textbook-brisk acidity.

🍷 9 **Casillero del Diablo Carmenère 2011**   £7.48
Runs the Cab Sauv (above) close for sheer enjoyability; a very dense and dark, plummy and creamy spin on the sleek Carmenère theme with 14% alcohol.

🍷 8 **Mayu Syrah Reserva 2007**   £8.48
A strong, rich red now showing its age but still relishable; 14% alcohol.

🍷 8 **Viñalba Malbec Syrah 2010**   £8.48
Dense and gripping Patagonian blend with 14.5% alcohol has lavish blackberry fruit, dark chocolate undertone and smooth integrity.

Red Wines

8 Asda Côtes du Rhône 2011　　　　　**£3.67**
Look at the price! It's light and leafy but wholesomely ripe.

9 Asda Beaujolais 2011　　　　　**£4.48**
Bright, purple, raspberry-nosed glugger with masses of juicy fruit and a good grip. You get a lot of flavour for your money.

8 Asda Claret　　　　　**£4.99**
It is of the humblest AC Bordeaux rank and of no stated vintage, but this is a firm and fully formed Merlot-led sunny and balanced claret of unimpeachable character.

8 La Maison Elyse Cabernet Sauvignon 2011 £5.98
Pays d'Oc sleek black-fruit food wine (try lamb dishes) has focused, satisfying ripeness and a crunchy dry finish.

**9 Extra Special Bordeaux Supérieur
Roc-Montalon 2010**　　　　　**£6.97**
Intense inky purple, long and dense in its structured black fruit, this is sinuous, silky and firm, with expensive sleekness, mint, cedar and plum. Lovely now, but it will mellow for years to come.

8 Extra Special Shiraz 2011　　　　　**£6.97**
Hearty Pays d'Oc spice bomb has a big cushion of peppery black fruit and a roasty ripeness; 14.5% alcohol. Adopting Australian 'Shiraz' for indigenous grape Syrah is absurd.

FRANCE

RED WINES

FRANCE

8 **The Original Malbec 2011**   £7.47
A tilt at Argentine imitators? This is butch and black enough to compete, with roasted fruit depths and a lick of caramel.

8 **Extra Special Crozes Hermitage 2009**   £8.37
Intense, spicy, blueberry-fruit northern Rhône classic at a sensible price; I liked this vintage better than the 2008, which was garlanded with medals.

8 **Celliers des Dauphins Vinsobres 2009**   £9.51
Elevated village Côtes du Rhône is a bulked-up variation on the pale, spicy theme with appreciable weight, maturity and alcohol (14%).

ITALY

8 **Asda Sicilian Red**   £3.98
Wholesome, heathery party red based on Sangiovese (the grape of Chianti) is a brambly bargain.

8 **Asda Chianti 2011**   £4.98
Tastes like Chianti – gently abrasive cherry-strawberry fruit with a dollop of cream and dry nutskin finish – but not overpriced as too much Chianti is. Bargain.

8 **Casa Lella Nero d'Avola 2011**   £5.68
Near-austere roasty-fruit Sicilian with a whiff of volcano (and 14% alcohol) has defined dry edge and will suit pasta dishes with spicy sauces very well.

9 **Extra Special Montepulciano
D'Abruzzo 2011**   £6.98
Tempting cassis nose and sweet-briar fruit in this rich-but-crunchy, thoroughly Italian red with a de luxe oak element; lively and lush.

RED WINES

ITALY

10 **Extra Special Chianti Classico Riserva 2008** **£7.98**
Ideal Chianti, darkly ripe and brimming with healthy, dark, savoury fruit in the traditional Tuscan juicy-grippy style, with purity and natural balance mellowed by the years. At this price it's a great bargain.

N. ZEALAND

10 **Extra Special New Zealand
Pinot Noir 2009** **£10.18**
The colour is turning, the nose is a bloom of pure Kiwi Pinot, sun-kissed cherries, the lot; the fruit follows up faithfully with sweet savour and perfect balance. Made by Wither Hills, it's a perfect expression of a unique wine style.

SOUTH AFRICA

8 **Asda Pinotage 2011** **£4.17**
Light in weight but by no means insubstantial (14.5% alcohol), this bargain has relishable tarry savour.

9 **Extra Special South African
Pinotage 2011** **£6.98**
Eager black-fruit Fairtrade wine grabs the tastebuds with its richness, pungency and juiciness and finishes with a neat acidity; it works so well.

SPAIN

7 **Asda Tempranillo** **£3.93**
Simple blackcurranty dry Valencian red is healthy and cheap.

9 **Torres Sangre de Toro 2010** **£5.13**
Suitably robust and muscular Catalan brand is consistently delicious and satisfying. Sold everywhere, but cheaper by a mile at Asda if this price prevails.

SPAIN

8   **Extra Special Old Vines Garnacha 2011**   £6.98
Fun, juicy but substantial (14% alcohol) and grippy red
from Carinena region with artful oak enhancement; good
paella match.

8   **Pilgrimage Mazuelo 2011**   £7.28
Clove and eucalyptus in this dark, oaked, slinky red from
Extremadura on the Portuguese border, with 14.5%
alcohol.

8   **Paul de Albas Ribero del Duero 2011**   £8.98
Sweet vanilla richness in this pure Tempranillo still gives
priority to the sinewy, minty-dark fruit; time will serve
this well.

10   **Noster Nobilis 2007**   £9.98
This gamey, truffly, plump and regally dense dark
Garnacha-based and thoroughly fabulous wine is from
the mysterious, cult-status denominación of Priorat in the
remote hills of Tarragona, west of Barcelona. Mature,
savoury and rich (14.5% alcohol) it is a great introduction
to Priorat and at under a tenner, a rare bird.

PINK WINES

France

🍷 **8** **Les Estivales Rosé 2011** £5.98
Fluorescent Languedoc food pink (try salad niçoise)
has wild strawberry perfume, lots of berry fruit (Syrah/
Grenache) and a very crisp edge.

Spain

🍷 **8** **Viña Sol Rosé 2011** £5.98
Bright magenta colour and equally bright red-berry fruit
in this dry, crisp pink from a famed Catalan producer.

🍷 **7** **Viña Albali Rosé 2011** £6.18
Big-brand La Mancha pink has lots of strawberry fruit
with a shameless sugar boost; fun, though.

WHITE WINES

Australia

🍷 **8** **De Bortoli Family Selection
Chardonnay 2011** £5.98
Spearmint and flint in this rather Chablis-like budget
Riverina dry white.

Chile

🍷 **8** **Mayu Pedro Ximenez 2011** £6.98
An emphatically dry wine from a grape more familiar
from sweet sherry, this is fresh with a hint of Muscat
grapes, subtle and likeable – a good salad matcher.

France

🍷 **10** **Asda Marsanne 2011** £4.47
Return to brilliance from this fascinating Pays d'Oc
varietal with lots of positive green/tropical fruit and a
keen edge. Made by giant Foncalieu, it is a force in value-
for-money quality wine; it works wonderfully well.

🍷 **8** **Etoile de Nuit Sauvignon Blanc 2011** £5.98
Cabbage-crisp Gascon dry refresher has asparagus
savour; likeable and 11.5% alcohol.

White Wines

FRANCE

🍷 8 Extra Special Chardonnay 2011   £6.98
Pays d'Oc oaked, crispy apple dry wine with a lick of peachy ripeness; this is France's answer to generic Aussie Chardy, and I like it.

🍷 8 Extra Special Viognier 2011   £7.07
There is suddenly of lot of fine, fresh Viognier from France. This has a green tang at entry followed up by fine preserved-fruit flavours (dates, apricots and more) en route to a dry, zippy finish.

🍷 8 Asda Petit Chablis 2010   £7.27
Plenty of Chablis character here, flinty, racy and recognisable.

**🍷 8 Extra Special Chablis Domaine de
       la Levée 2010**   £9.34
Alluring gold colour and creamy intensity in this generous and long-flavoured typical Chablis by well-regarded Domaines Brocard.

🍷 8 Extra Special Pouilly Fumé 2010   £10.78
Plush, leesy, posh Loire Sauvignon is fresh rather than green, and good value for this appellation.

ITALY

🍷 8 Asda Sicilian White   £4.12
Sweet, nutty nose on this non-vintage party white by giant Settesoli co-op is followed up by breezy orchard fruits.

🍷 8 Extra Special Soave Classico 2011   £5.98
Attractive lemon-gold colour and a nifty balance of blanched-almond richness and herbaceous white fruit in this respectable Verona dry white.

WHITE WINES

ITALY

🍷 **8** **Extra Special Falanghina 2011** £6.48
Lemon twang in this nutty-grassy Puglian dry white.

🍷 **8** **Extra Special Pinot Grigio 2011** £6.98
Trentino product is a definite step up from average, with minerality and pungency.

N. ZEALAND

🍷 **9** **Tukituki Sauvignon Blanc 2011** £4.48
A new phenomenon, cheap Kiwi wine, and this one, from Marlborough, belies its price: nettly-fresh, pleasing typical fruit, and gentle acidity.

🍷 **9** **Extra Special Sauvignon Blanc 2010** £7.48
Minty-raspberry-seagrass-scented lusciously fruity Marlborough wine by redoubtable Wither Hills winery is special indeed – and good value.

S. AFRICA

🍷 **8** **Garden Route Chenin Blanc 2011** £7.98
Brisk aroma and rich fruit in this cunning contrivance of a dry refresher with both honey and zest.

SPAIN

🍷 **8** **Asda Moscatel de Valencia** £4.13
Honeyed, but not sickly, fortified (15% alcohol) birthday-cake wine to serve well chilled in small measures.

🍷 **9** **Villa Ludy Albariño 2011** £7.48
Generous colour and healthy cabbage-patch whiff to this glorious Sauvignon-style grassy dry white from the Rias Baixas in Galicia; long, seaside-fresh, contemplative classic.

Asda

SPARKLING WINES

FRANCE

🍷 8 **Louis Bernard Champagne Brut** £21.98
Soft, mellow Pinot-Meunier-dominated champagne has mouthfilling mousse and immediate attraction; look out for this one on discount.

🍷 9 **Extra Special Louis Bernard Vintage Champagne 2004** £24.97
Successor to the brilliant ES 2002 Champagne, this is worthy: toasty whiff, rich, nuanced fruit, artful freshness, and a lot of mature charm for the money.

ITALY

🍷 8 **Extra Special Prosecco** £9.97
With sweet elderflower nose and peary fruit, it balances well and turns out just off-dry.

SPAIN

🍷 7 **Asda Mas Miralda Semi-sec Cava** £4.48
It's not all that sweet, and I like it better than Asti (though at 13% it's about twice the ABV); a bargain of a kind at the price.

🍷 9 **Asda Cava Rosada** £4.63
Smoked salmon in colour, eagerly fizzy and powerfully scented with strawberry, this busy Catalan sparkler is amazing value.

🍷 8 **Extra Special Vintage Cava 2010** £9.98
Yeasty-creamy nose, fruit ripe rather than sweet, crisply fresh, it's made with oaked Chardonnay in the blend.

Co-op

Disaster struck. I missed the Co-op's always-excellent tasting. Transport difficulties, to put it mildly. So, with apologies both to the readers and to the wine team at the Co-op, this year's entry is a token one. The few wines that follow are those I have lately tried from among my own purchases.

RED WINES

ARGENTINA

♉9 Finca Mirador Shiraz 2009 £6.49
Deep purple, lavishly oaked blackberry-pie mouthfiller is juicy and long with 14% alcohol. Good value.

AUSTRALIA

♉8 St Hallett Shiraz 2008 £8.99
Reliable ripe Barossa wine mellowing nicely from oak contact and a few years in bottle.

CHILE

**♉8 Trio Merlot/Carmenère/
Cabernet Sauvignon 2010** £7.99
Convincing three-way blend from Chilean giant Concha y Toro is dark, smooth and grippy.

FRANCE

♉8 Palais des Anciens Côtes du Rhône 2009 £7.49
Grippingly good spicy-savoury wine from a great Rhône vintage.

ITALY

**♉8 The Co-operative Premium Valpolicella
Ripasso 2009** £7.99
The Co-op takes a first tentative step into upmarket wine branding with, among others, this nice juicy Veronese specialty red; good, intense cherry red with grip.

WHITE WINES

AUSTRALIA

🍷 8 **The Co-operative Jacaranda Hill Semillon Chardonnay 2011** £4.89

I liked this peachy-pineapple refresher from the Riverina, bought at an eye-catching discount for £3.99. Look out for a repeat.

CHILE

🍷 8 **Trio Chardonnay/Pinot Grigio/ Pinot Blanc 2010** £7.99

Surprisingly enjoyable if unlikely blend by Concha y Toro is dry with tropical fruitiness and a lemon twang. I paid a discount £5.99, which is nearer the value.

FRANCE

🍷 8 **The Co-operative Chablis 2010** £9.49

Vivid mineral proper Chablis from ubiquitous merchant Brocard is notably fresh and brisk.

GERMANY

🍷 8 **Devil's Rock Riesling 2011** £6.49

Dry Rheinpfalz wine looks Australian but it's in the modern German style, fermented out, racy, limey and bright.

ITALY

🍷 9 **Rocca Vecchia Falanghina 2010/11** £5.99

The 2010, still on shelf, was a top wine last year and I would put money on the 2011, but haven't tasted it. Lovely long, lush, dry style from Puglia.

N. ZEALAND

🍷 8 **The Co-operative Explorer's Vineyard Sauvignon Blanc 2011** £8.79

Generous gooseberry-and-nettles formula makes this a consistently good buy.

WHITE WINES

SPAIN

🍷 8 Viña Sol 2011   £6.99

Another good vintage for this enduring Catalan brand: crisp orchard fruit, lemon zest, as sunny as it sounds. Sold everywhere, but Co-ops regularly discount it to £4.99.

SPARKLING WINE

FRANCE

🍷 9 Les Pionniers Brut   £17.99

The Co-op's house champagne is consistently friendly, with the right mix of the mellow and the fresh; 90% Pinot (70 Noir, 20 Meunier), it has the strawberry ripeness you might look for in pink champagne, but rarely find.

Majestic

 I love the wines at Majestic, but I do have a problem with the prices. Most of the wines appear to be on promotion, most of the time. It's even worse than the supermarkets. Majestic operates a minimum-purchase policy of six bottles, any mix, so you are compelled to 'multibuy'. Doesn't this obviate the need for 'buy two, save 20 per cent' promotions?

My guess is that the real value Majestic places on its wines is usually the discounted price. The company, I reckon, assumes no customer will be mad enough to pay £11.99 for one bottle of Nicolas Potel's fabulous Bourgogne Pinot Noir Vieilles Vignes 2010 (which I hope will still be on promo now) when two bottles can be had for £8.99 apiece.

In this case, fair enough. I wouldn't hesitate to buy two bottles of this wine, funds permitting. I have tasted it and believe it's well worth £8.99. But for customers browsing the canyons of cases that crowd the warehouse-like branches, there must be moments of hesitation in front of totally unfamiliar wines. Risking one bottle is brave; risking two might be foolhardy.

This is not a problem with generic promotions. Perpetually, you can save 20 per cent per bottle if you buy any two wines from several different nations and/ or regions. That brings hundreds of individual wines within discount reach.

And again, I must be fair. Majestic is a serious wine merchant, and consequently sells few, if any, bad wines. You're really quite safe. While the supermarkets persist in offering horrible global brands on the hard-to-refute grounds that these are what their customers want, Majestic appears to choose its wines on the even-harder-to-refute grounds that they're good. What's more, you won't find them anywhere else. The few brands Majestic does sell seem consistently to be of the better kind.

There is a good website, but I still prefer to peruse the printed lists Majestic sends out four times a year. All the wines are there, and details of all the promotions too. Given how numerous and complex they all are, it's a good idea to swot up a bit before you shop.

RED WINES

8 **Lunta Malbec 2010** £12.99
Sinewy but brambly and friendly Mendoza is darkly rich and balanced; 14% alcohol.

8 **Luca Malbec 2009** £21.99
If for some reason you just have to have a premium Argentine red, this one should do; bold, black fruit tempered by age and new oak has de luxe feel and textbook balance; 14% alcohol.

ARGENTINA

8 **Peter Lehmann EVS Shiraz 2010** £12.49
Hefty (14.5% alcohol) but trim, bold, spicy Eden Valley red has keen citrus edge.

8 **Wirra Wirra Church Block Cabernet Shiraz Merlot 2010** £12.49
Gamey-ripe blend has a whiff of leather followed by a whack of defined rich cassis-and-spice black fruit; 14.5% alcohol.

AUSTRALIA

8 **LFE Signature Series Syrah Reserva 2010** £7.99
Healthy and finely weighted spice-and-plum ripe Central Valley wine at a reasonable standard price; 14% alcohol.

8 **Anakena Single Vineyard Deu Pinot Noir 2011** £9.99
Leafy/green pepper nose on this punchy Leyda Valley Pinot.

8 **Tabali Reserva Carmenère 2010** £9.99
Dense carmine colour – well, purple, really – to this muscular deep-fruited and creamy-oaked Colchagua keeping wine, with 14.5% alcohol.

CHILE

RED WINES

8 Côté Mas Rouge 2011   £6.99
Bumper Pays d'Oc has savoury, spicy ripeness.

9 Pinot Noir La Grille 2010   £6.99
Russet-red colour and a beamish cherry nose proclaim
this charming Saint Pourçain (Loire) refresher to serve
cool with fish or fowl.

9 Laurent Miquel L'Artisan Faugères 2010 £7.99
Coal-dark Languedoc heavyweight has matching core
of roasty flavour with spice and briar from Syrah and
Grenache grapes. Every inch a Faugères.

8 Beaujolais Château de Pizay 2011   £8.74
Startling mauve colour gives way to a juicy, raspy fruit of
real charm.

8 Château La Dournie St Chinian 2009   £8.99
Rather refined dark-fruit (Syrah-based) spice bomb with
blackberry juiciness.

8 Domaine Les Yeuses Les Epices Syrah 2009 £8.99
Toasty-roasty intense black-fruit Pays d'Oc is very ripe
but by no means cooked. Needs meat.

8 Côtes du Rhône Vidal Fleury 2010   £9.99
Looks good, tastes vibrant, spicy and complete; 14%
alcohol.

8 Lirac Domaine des Garrigues 2011   £9.99
Young, still tannic, but showing lots of gutsy, spicy
promise.

RED WINES

FRANCE

7 **Morgon Château de Pizay 2011** £9.99
Densely coloured, big, grippy Beaujolais is far too young for now, but shows promise for two years hence.

9 **Bourgogne Pinot Noir Vieilles Vignes
Nicolas Potel 2010** £11.99
Looks light, but this bloomingly perfumed, raspberry-ripe red has creaminess, even a lick of caramel, and sweet juiciness galore.

9 **Les Hauts de Castelmaure Corbières 2009** £11.99
This smooth, beguiling, part-new-oaked variation on the usually rugged Corbières model is very appealing indeed; 14% alcohol, it needs starchy, meaty food.

8 **Lirac Vignobles Abeille 2010** £14.99
From Châteauneuf estate Mont Redon, a grand Châteauneuf-style wine with complex structure in a firm texture (14% alcohol). Keep as long as you can.

ITALY

8 **Rosso Piceno Conte Saladino 2010** £8.74
Bouncing cherry-fruit Marches red has a lick of richness and a clean, dry finish.

9 **Surani Costarossa Primitivo
di Manduria 2010** £9.99
Exotic, truffly, black-fruit, sweet-briar, gamey monster (14.5% alcohol) of great character; needs grilled meat.

8 **Masi Campofiorin 2008** £12.49
Iconic ripasso-like Verona (Valpolicella) red is slick, roasty, mellow and richly briary.

RED WINES

ITALY

8 Poliziano Rosso di Montepulciano 2010 £14.99
At an unusually reasonable price for this Tuscan classic, this is a deliciously dark and savoury example with 14% alcohol.

NEW ZEALAND

10 The Ned Pinot Noir 2010 £12.49
A huge Marlborough (Waihopai River) Pinot with deep, developed, summer-pudding fruit finished with grip and tang. A wine of utterly convincing naturalness and completeness, and 14% alcohol.

9 Villa Maria Private Bin Syrah 2009 £12.49
The contrast with most Aussie Syrah/Shiraz is extraordinary: this is elegant and sleek, spicy and powerful, all at once.

8 Giesen Pinot Noir 2010 £13.74
Lush, green, leafy tang in this light-but-tight summer-soft-fruit red in the true Kiwi eucalypt style.

PORTUGAL

8 Alentejo Ramos Reserva 2011 £8.49
Agreeably abrasive minty-juicy midweight to go with grilled sardines; thoroughly Portuguese.

9 Churchill Estates Douro 2008 £10.99
Porty perfume and luscious minty-dark fruit in this faithful table red from the port country.

10 Quinta da Bacalhôa 2008 £13.49
An old friend suddenly rematerialises, as gorgeous as ever. From Setubal it's a dark, minty Cabernet Sauvignon, aged a year in new oak, with notes of cassis, cloves and tobacco. It's 14.5% alcohol and there's no other Cabernet like it.

RED WINES

8 La Garnacha Salvaje del Moncayo 2010 £9.99
Big, sweet, brambly glugger has a lot of rustic charm and
eager freshness; from the northern end of the Ebro Valley.

8 Matsu El Picaro Toro 2011 £9.99
One of a series of Toro wines labelled with eye-catching
photos of gnarled blokes wearing cloth caps, this has
appropriately butch hedgerow fruit, softened with oak.

8 Rioja Reserva Viña Eguia 2006 £9.99
Easy weight, creamy vanilla oak and vigorously healthy
blackcurrant fruit in fine balance.

8 Alvaro Palacios Camins del Priorat 2010 £17.49
An introduction to the cult Priorat region, this is 14.5%
alcohol and delivers a big burst of plummy, super-ripe,
spicy fruit in a sleek, smooth package.

10 Viña Ardanza Rioja Reserva Especial 2001 £22.00
I guessed it might be over the hill, but this is a defining
wine from a great Rioja Alta estate in the best possible
vintage. Vivid fruit and perfectly pitched vanilla richness
in a world-class wine that is well worth the money.

SPAIN

9 Chateau Ste Michelle Merlot 2007 £12.99
Beautifully weighted Washington State oaked wine with
black-cherry richness and perfectly poised acidity; elegant
and exciting.

8 Cline Ancient Vines Zinfandel 2010 £19.99
Zinfandel followers should like this new-oaked, prickly-
bright, dark-fruited blockbuster with 15% alcohol.

USA

PINK WINES

9 La Grille Pinot Noir Rosé 2011 £6.99
Coral-coloured Loire pink has proper Pinot character and
abounding freshness.

8 Domaine La Chautarde Rosé 2011 £8.99
Pale salmon colour to this sensibly priced Provence pink;
sunny-briar (Grenache) fruit with crisp edge.

8 Château Pigoudet La Chapelle Rosé 2011 £9.99
Pale, crisp, firm, dry and full of summer fruit flavours,
from Provence.

8 Famille Abeille Rosé 2011 £10.99
Pale magenta Provence pink has a sweet background to
the fresh and lively dry, upfront fruit. Neatly contrived.

8 Châteu Barthès Rosé Bandol 2011 £11.99
Shocking pink and correspondingly impactful in fruitiness,
this big, briary pink from a fashionable Mediterranean
spot is satisfying and stimulating.

8 AIX Rosé 2011 1.5 litre £19.99
Stately magnum bottle for parties delivers an easy, fresh,
flowery Coteaux d'Aix en Provence pink with coral
colour and firm fruit.

8 Fairleigh Estate Pinot Noir Rosé 2011 £7.49
Bold cherry-raspberry Pinot fruit in this onion-skin-
coloured, crisp and satisfying Marlborough pink.

8 Villa Maria Private Bin Rosé 2011 £8.74
Magenta Merlot/Malbec melange has sweet-cherry nose
but a dry, citrus-brisk and zingy fruit. Lush and fresh.

WHITE WINES

8 **Viñalba Seleccion Torrontes 2011** £9.99
Nice dry-Muscatty rasp in this fresh, dry charmer from
Argentina's national white grape.

8 **DB Reserve Chardonnay 2010** £9.49
Relishable buttery-but-brisk, fresh and delicate wine
from De Bortoli.

8 **The Lodge Hill Riesling 2011** £12.49
From Jim Barry in the Clare Valley, a restrained, mineral-
limey food wine of real power.

8 **Yalumba Viognier 2010** £13.74
Spare, near-austere dry and apricotty Eden Valley wine
has an authentic rush of fruit.

7 **Shadowfax Chardonnay 2010** £25.00
Not from New Zealand's Lord of the Rings country but
from Mornington, Victoria, a rich, Beaune-like confection
for Tolkienites.

8 **LFE Gran Reserva Chardonnay 2011** £9.99
Sweet-apple style, very ripe (14% alcohol) but artfully
fresh Casablanca dry food wine (poultry).

9 **Leyda Single Vineyard Chardonnay 2009** £10.99
Yellow, old-fashioned, near-oxidative, 14% alcohol,
sublimely balanced – I loved it.

8 **La Grille Touraine Sauvignon Blanc 2011** £7.49
Floral nose, easy acidity and generous seagrass fruit in
this simple Loire refresher.

WHITE WINES

8 Mâcon Blanc Les Pierres Blanches 2011 £7.99
One of very few likeable Mâcons I've tried from 2011, this is yellow, soft and peachy.

8 Monte Vallon Chardonnay 2011 £7.99
Nutty, leesy and beguiling dry Pays d'Oc has sweet-apple allure.

8 Château de Cléray Muscadet de Sèvre et Maine Sur Lie 2011 £8.99
Fresh and twangy (but not over-acid) de luxe variation on the classic Loire mussel matcher.

8 Mâcon-Villages Les Roches Blanches 2010 £9.99
From big merchant Louis Jadot, a maturing, sunny Chardonnay with long, plush flavour, minerality and citrus edge.

8 Sancerre Les Baudrières 2011 £10.99
Grapefruit twist in this reasonably priced Loire classic gives it a lift above the bog standard.

8 Alsace Gewürztraminer Les Princes Abbés 2009 £15.99
Big, yellow wine by Schlumberger burgeons with lychee perfume and ripe tropical fruits, with a citrus trim.

8 Riesling Kabinett Trocken Prinz von Hessen 2009 £10.99
Mineral-crisp 'dry' (fermented out) Rheingau wine of impressive purity.

WHITE WINES

ITALY

♈ 7 **Serena Pinot Grigio 2011** £8.74
Smartly packaged Tuscan PG has plenty of ripeness and interest.

♈ 8 **Contesa Pecorino 2011** £9.99
Odd children's-scribble label reveals a nicely defined, tangy, dry Abruzzo wine of grassy lushness.

♈ 8 **Roero Arneis Marco Porello 2011** £9.99
Piedmont dry wine has candied-orchard-fruit aroma and a plump but eagerly fresh body of flavour.

♈ 8 **Vermentino Poggioargentiera 2011** £9.99
Blanched almonds, sweet pear and a faint pétillance highlight this intriguing Tuscan dry wine. Elegant but sturdy food matcher (chicken, fish, pasta).

♈ 9 **Vernaccia di San Gimignano
A Passoni 2011** £9.99
Tuscan tourist favourite has a flinty twang that elevates the aromatic, orchardy fruit. Terrific.

NEW ZEALAND

♈ 9 **Giesen Sauvignon Blanc 2011** £8.74
Wildly lush, grassy-nettly Marlborough almost fizzes with freshness and crispness. At promo price (£5.99–£6.99), very keen value.

♈ 9 **The Ned Sauvignon Blanc 2011** £8.74
Ubiquitous Marlborough wine is river-fresh (the river Waihopai in this case), with a stony minerality, basketfuls of ripe white fruits, and even a tang of blackcurrant.

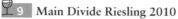

White Wines

NEW ZEALAND

🍷 9 **Main Divide Riesling 2010**   £12.49
Ripe, limey, Pegasus Bay, Waipara, contrivance is racy and gorgeous, and 11.5% alcohol.

🍷 8 **The King's Thorn Pinot Gris 2011**   £12.49
Big, smoky, dry Marlborough wine has an agreeable pungency that transcends the peculiar packaging.

🍷 8 **Saint Clair Pioneer Block
       Chardonnay 2009**   £16.99
Yellow, leesy Marlborough dry wine combines richness and flintiness in such a distinctively Kiwi way; 14% alcohol.

SPAIN

🍷 10 **Caixas Albariño Rias Baixas 2011**   £9.99
Simply perfect seagrass and white-fruit dry wine from the redoubtable Martin Codax of Rias Baixas on the west coast; flavour is long, luxuriant and unforgettable.

🍷 9 **Montenovo Godello 2010**   £9.99
From Godello grapes grown in the Galician DO of Valdeorras, a fascinating dry, sunnily herbaceous white with a seductive honey background; lovely balance.

SPARKLING WINES

ENGLAND

8 Chapel Down Pinot Reserve 2005   **£23.99**
Lively Home Counties sparkler has ritzy small-bubble mousse and keenly defined fruit. Really rather good.

9 Nyetimber Classic Cuvée 2004   **£29.99**
Forgiveably expensive vintage Sussex sparkler from Champagne cépage has an elegant bloom, mellow mouthfeel and convincing freshness.

FRANCE

8 Comte De Lamotte Champagne Brut   **£15.00**
This is cheap champagne even at the standard price, and it's not at all bad, with a digestive-biscuit whiff and brisk fruit.

8 Montaudon Champagne Brut   **£17.00**
Another (relatively) cheap and cheerful champers that seems to have some bottle-age and a hint of richness.

8 Oeil de Perdrix Rosé Champagne Brut   **£25.00**
Its name, meaning 'eye of partridge', is supposed to describe the bold pink colour; a dry but nicely strawberry-nuanced fizz only found at Majestic.

8 Laurent Perrier Champagne Rosé Brut   **£55.00**
Non-vintage but widely bruited as the best of pink champagnes, this is truly pink-tasting, with summer soft fruit of surpassing freshness. At a discount from the shocking standard price this is a worthwhile major treat.

—Marks & Spencer—

 It all looks good at M&S. Highlights include some delicious and well-priced Italian reds, bargains from Chile, a fabulous claret and a sparkling English wine that makes me think that our home-grown fizz industry might truly be coming of age.

Don't expect to find all the wines covered here in every M&S branch. Some will be in the biggest stores only, although even larger branches, in my experience, can have a pretty limited range. The biggest selection is to be found online at M&S Wine Direct, where everything is available for home delivery in six-bottle cases.

There are usually a few wines on promotion in the stores, but the best bargains tend to be online, with regular reductions of 25 per cent off six-bottle cases from particular countries and, occasionally, off the entire range. It pays to be vigilant.

RED WINES

♈ 7 Rincón del Sol Red 2011 £4.99
Bright, perky Bonarda/Merlot split has juicy fruit.

♈ 8 El Esteco Tannat 2011 £6.99
Blood-red, endearingly oaked, simple sunny wine from the world's healthiest grape variety.

♈ 8 Viñalta Malbec 2011 £7.49
Plump, unoaked, well-judged, leather-sheeny Mendoza wine from Argentina's keynote grape; 14.5% alcohol.

♈ 8 Fairtrade Monteflores Malbec 2011 £9.99
Superior, discreetly oaked, savoury black-fruit classic Fairtrade Malbec is 14.5% alcohol and has a future.

ARGENTINA

♈ 8 Barossa Valley Petit Verdot 2010 £9.99
Prunes and loganberry feature in a comfortably toasty wine with Bordeaux pretensions and lots of dark charm.

♈ 9 Coonawarra Cabernet Sauvignon 2010 £9.99
Dramatically dense and gloopy-looking monster has the legs of a cavalry troop and a fine, dark-hearted, cassis-mint-spice medley of flavours with 14% alcohol; in fact, the weight is perfectly judged.

♈ 8 Tractor Tube Society Malbec 2010 £13.99
From Zonte's Footstep in the Clare Valley, a friendly, silky and spicy 14% alcohol classic oaked Malbec that's worth the investment.

♈ 9 Mattiske Road Shiraz 2010 £16.99
Roast-beef red, it will even stand up to the horseradish. Pure, plump, perfect long-new-oaked Cornas-like luxury red with 15% alcohol.

AUSTRALIA

RED WINES

♈ 9 Soleado Cabernet Sauvignon 2011 £5.49
Beguiling, classic, smoothie Chilean Cabernet with savoury fruit and gentle grip – great value.

**♈ 9 Canelo Fairtrade Cabernet Sauvignon
Carmenère 2010** £6.99
I am hugely in favour of Fairtrade wines but do worry about quality. This one shines, with its hearty, rounded, dark minty-cassis fruit, slightly tough tannin (time will soften) and long tail.

♈ 8 CM Carmenère 2011 £7.49
Dense and toasty meat-matching Elqui-region monster has a de luxe leather whiff and dark, savoury, black-fruit heart; 14.5% alcohol.

♈ 8 Cerro Syrah 2009 £7.99
Lots of spice and extract in this summer-pudding-scented, ultra-ripe, muscular Andean red. Strong medicine, with 14.5% alcohol.

♈ 9 Carignan Old Vineyard 2008 £11.99
Liquorice, coffee and treacle (it says here) are among the building blocks of this bold, dark edifice from the Carignan grape of France's Midi. Massive (14.5% alcohol), but elegantly weighty and clean-finishing.

♈ 9 Plan de Dieu Côtes du Rhône Villages 2010 £7.99
Instantly likeable for its rustic juicy ripeness and lively brambly gush of fruit, this is gloriously generous and satisfying.

CHILE

FRANCE

RED WINES

10 Héritage de Pierre Lurton 2009 £10.99

Great claret crops up in unexpected places. This is humble right-bank Merlot (with 20% Cabernet Sauvignon), but is dense, dark and ideally ripe (13.5% alcohol), with chocolate richness and intense black-cherry fruit. It would pass for a classed growth and is a bargain.

8 Moulin à Vent Domaine du Petit Chêne 2010 £12.99

Wee bit of barley sugar in the creamy-raspberry whiff from this top-of-the-range Beaujolais. It's a lush mix of bounce and silk, and will go on for years.

8 Domaine Bunan Bandol 2007 £14.99

Brooding, dark, super-ripe (14.5% alcohol) Côte d'Azur classic has a relishable prune-coffee whiff and plummy depths.

8 Sancerre Benoit Brochard Rouge 2009 £14.99

It's usually a mystery to me that anyone bothers with this Loire oddity from Pinot Noir but this one, at a price, works well: nice garnet colour, sweet earthy perfume, mineral strawberry plump poised fruit. Class act.

7 Palataia Pinot Noir 2011 £8.99

I'm not confident everyone will like this as much as I do, thus the cautious score. Only a degree darker than rosé, it has a natural earthy-cherry Pinot pong and poised, delicate summer fruit (with 13.5% alcohol). Rarefied and delightful.

FRANCE

GERMANY

RED WINES

9 Popolino Rosso 2011 £4.99

Old friend from Sicily is grippy and briary, fresh and juicy. Seems to have lost a little weight from earlier vintages, but still a true bargain thirst-quencher.

9 Reggiano Rosso 2011 £5.99

This is delicious still Lambrusco, from the grapes of that name, bramble and violet scented, juicy and raspingly fresh to drink cool.

8 Sangiovese di Romagna 2010 £5.99

A Chianti-style middleweight from the Romagna region, south of Tuscany, makes a likeable substitute with brisk fruit.

8 Sicilian Shiraz 2011 £5.99

Deeply coloured, intense black-fruit gripper has a long, juicy tail to the flavour. Will stand up well to pasta with chilli.

8 Chianti Colli di Rasenna 2010 £6.99

Sweet-smelling, ripe cherry-bramble, authentic spaghetti wine has proper nutskin finish; good price, for Chianti.

7 Nelson Malbec 2011 £9.99

Ethereal compared to, say, Mendoza counterparts, this is light in weight (but 14.5% in alcohol) with trademark Kiwi sleek mintiness.

9 Nelson Pinot Noir 2010 £9.99

Spot on. A big strawberry fruitiness with a sprinkle of pepper in this tastebud-grabbing food red. Great Kiwi Pinot from the redoubtable Seifried Estate (14% alcohol).

ITALY

NEW ZEALAND

RED WINES

S. AFRICA

🍷 8 **Houdamond Pinotage 2009** £9.49
Restrained, recognisable Stellenbosch tarry-savoury, intense, lavishly oaked, minty smoothie with 14.5% alcohol and a nice clean edge.

USA

🍷 10 **Home Ranch Pinot Noir 2009** £9.99
Pale colour going orange, this turned out to be a lovely sunny wine with earthy-cherry sweetness (and 14.5% alcohol), and elegant but friendly firmness. Superb.

PINK WINES

CHILE

🍷 8 **Casa Leona Rosé 2011** £6.99
Healthy onion-skin colour and plenty of crisp cassis fruit in this generous Cabernet-based food matcher.

ENGLAND

🍷 8 **English Rosé 2011** £10.99
It looks and smells like Pinot Noir, its majority (65%) constituent, and tastes crisply and freshly likewise. A rare, if expensive, treat from Chapel Down in Kent.

ITALY

🍷 7 **Vino d'Italia Rosé litre** £5.99
Cheap (litre price equals £4.49 per 75cl) non-vintage has pretty coral colour and pleasing soft summer fruit.

SPAIN

🍷 7 **Las Falleras Rosé 2011** £4.79
Lurid magenta colour, lick of strawberry, dry context, agreeable freshness.

🍷 8 **Bellota Rosado 2011** £5.99
Shocking-pink, hearty, blackcurrant, fruit-juicy mouthfiller is fresh and keen.

WHITE WINES

ARGENTINA

♇ 8 Rincón del Sol Chardonnay-Chenin Blanc 2011 £4.99

Sweet orchardy scent and matching fruit against a honey background in this refreshing dry confection.

♇ 8 La Finca Pinot Grigio 2011 £6.99

Smoky, exotic vegetal fruit in a briskly dry package.

AUSTRALIA

♇ 8 Yalumba Vermentino 2011 £9.99

South Australian spin on a Sardinian original is extra-ripe, herbaceous, rich yet dry, and 11.5% alcohol.

♇ 8 Xanadu Chardonnay 2011 £16.99

Gracefully oaked Margaret River pure-gold style with winning minerality and poise. A safe bet.

CHILE

♇ 8 Soleado Sauvignon Blanc 2011 £5.49

Tangy, grassy and brisk, this cheapie has a lick of residual sugar to please the crowd.

♇ 8 Eclipse Riesling 2011 £7.99

Limey and mouthfilling, dry and mineral, emphatically New World riesling is food wine (poultry, fish) from giant Cono Sur winery.

FRANCE

♇ 8 Gers Blanc 2011 £4.79

Basic price but a more-than-basic Colombard/Ugni refresher with 11.5% alcohol and plenty of sunny ripeness.

♇ 7 Domaine Mandeville Sauvignon Blanc 2011 £7.49

Ripe gooseberry, soft-finishing Languedoc glugger in a plastic bottle.

WHITE WINES

8 **Vouvray Domaine de la Pouvraie 2010**   £8.99
Jauntily rhyming, dry-but-lush Loire Chenin Blanc is 11.5% alcohol, but delivers a nice basket of fruit and great balance.

7 **Alsace Gewürztraminer 2011**   £9.49
From the ubiquitous Turckheim co-op, with rich colour and a lot of lychee perfume, this is plump and a shade sweet.

9 **Burgundy Chardonnay 2009**   £9.99
Humble-seeming AC Bourgogne comes from Chassagne-Montrachet, and tastes like it: a gold-coloured, creamy but discreetly oaked, ripe sweet-apple, proper burgundy with minerality and balance.

8 **Chablis Domaine Pierre de Préhy 2008**   £13.99
Nicely evolved, mature gold wine in the rich burgundy tradition but with the characteristic flinty minerality of proper Chablis. A tad pricy, but lovely.

8 **St Aubin 1er Cru Domaine
Les Chamois 2008**   £22.00
Neighbour of Montrachet and credibly so, this is a luscious balancing act between thrillingly defined Chardonnay of butter-rich ripeness, and citrus acidity.

8 **Palataia Pinot Grigio 2011**   £7.99
Strong, smoky and mineral, this assertive dry Rhine wine is more focused than most Italian counterparts.

White Wines

10 Falanghina Beneventano 2011 £5.99

Blanched nuts and lemons in harmony here, either side of a nice green brassica fruit with genteel ripeness; a super-value, fresh dry white from the Campania.

7 Pinot Grigio Bidoli 2011 £7.49

Lemon edge builds interest in this frisky Friuli PG.

8 Quadro Sei Gavi 2011 £7.49

Almondy lush Piedmont dry white is generous and elegant.

9 Nelson Sauvignon Blanc 2011 £9.49

The world's awash with Sauvignon but this Seifried Estate production still stands out: green grass, pure big-fruit lushness and contemplative depths.

8 Earth's End Riesling 2009 £12.99

Central Otago wine surprised me with its Moselle-like raciness and weight (though it's 13.5% alcohol). Delicious.

8 Single Block Series S1 Sauvignon Blanc 2011 £12.99

Nettles on the nose and a lovely zingy rush of grass and goosegog in the mouth. Only in 56 branches.

7 Tapada de Villar Vinho Verde 2011 £6.99

Very pale, slightly spritzy and abrading with some nice white fruit in front of a crisp finish; 11% alcohol.

ITALY

NEW ZEALAND

PORTUGAL

WHITE WINES

🍷 8 Ken Forrester Chenin Blanc 2011 £7.99

Dry, mineral style might make you wonder if it's Riesling, but this is trademark Forrester Chenin (of a kind familiar under other retailer labels) and a good salad matcher. It's 14% alcohol.

🍷 9 Villiera Traditional Barrel Fermented Chenin Blanc 2011 £10.99

Hugely ripe (14% alcohol) and rich-oaked, yellow, special-occasion Stellenbosch with honeysuckle notes balanced by artful limey acidity is a real attention-grabber. Aperitif, or to match paté, creamy pastas, poultry.

SPARKLING WINES

🍷 8 Sparkling English Brut £20.00

Mostly Pinots from southeast England, a vigorous Chapel Down wine with a mellow biscuity glow.

🍷 10 English Sparkling Rosé £22.00

This is not pink, it's gold, and it doesn't taste pink to me either, but I loved it. From six parts Pinot Noir and Meunier to four of Chardonnay and a couple of German varieties, it is an out-and-out tilt at champagne: creamy, toasty, bright and thrillingly made by Chapel Down in Kent. Flawless.

🍷 9 Marksman English Sparkling Brut Blanc de Blancs 2009 £22.00

Ridgeview (Sussex) Chardonnay is on target with focused, tangy-but-creamy and properly appley fruit. English fizz is beginning to live up to its prices.

SOUTH AFRICA

ENGLAND

Marks & Spencer

SPARKLING WINES

FRANCE

8 Champagne Desroches Brut £25.00
Well-coloured, mellow brioche, mature-tasting champagne is substantial and satisfying.

8 Oudinot Champagne Brut 2005 £28.00
Nicely rounded pure Chardonnay is mellow and mouthfilling.

ITALY

8 Prosecco Zardetto £11.99
Pale, peary and prodigiously fizzy, this is quite dry, though the orchard fruit is appreciably ripe.

N. ZEALAND

8 Mount Bluff Sauvignon Blanc Brut £10.99
Zingy elderflower nose and true grassy gooseberry Sauvignon fruit in this carbonated Marlborough blend with Chardonnay. Curiously likeable.

SPAIN

8 Pinot Noir Rosado Cava 2009 £12.99
Deep onion-skin colour and a proper blast of soft-summer-fruit Pinot give this characterful fizz a genuine edge. It's not cheap (for cava), but it is distinctively delicious.

7 Single Estate Chardonnay Cava 2009 £12.99
As sort of Catalan blanc de blancs, this really does taste like sparkling Chardonnay, though more like cava than champagne.

Morrisons

I have not had the chance to attend a tasting of the range from Morrisons this year in spite of the polite pleadings I made with head office. So this is a revisit to an earlier tasting, updated with purchases from my local branch in Somerset, which has lately been radically revamped, moving the wine department from a rather dark corner of the building to a bright and alluring position in the very centre of the store.

Perhaps this presages further improvements in the Morrisons wine range. After last year's great leap forward, with the introduction of a three-tiered range of own-label wines, I am optimistic. But for the moment, there is little further to report.

RED WINES

Morrisons

ARGENTINA

🍷 8 Trivento Reserve Syrah Malbec 2010   **£8.19**
Near-black blend makes the most of the spicy Shiraz and the dark, leathery savour of the Malbec; serious, satisfying red-meat wine with 14% alcohol.

AUSTRALIA

**🍷 9 Morrisons Australian Shiraz
Cabernet Sauvignon**   **£4.99**
A familiar blend, but this one is unusual: blended from more than one vintage, it has come out marvellously mellow and wholesome, with genial spice and relishable juicy dark fruit. Underpriced by a mile.

**🍷 9 Morrisons The Best McLaren Vale
Australian Shiraz 2007**   **£8.69**
From its dense, mature-looking ruby colour through the opulent, high-toned nose and into the depths of the juicy-spicy-toasty intense black fruit, this Geoff Merrill wine is hefty (14.5% alcohol), but poised, elegant and uplifting.

CHILE

🍷 8 Morrisons Chilean Carmenère 2010   **£6.99**
A dark and ripe centre in this long and toasty-oaked blackberry red will make it a nifty match for rare beef.

FRANCE

🍷 8 Morrisons French Cabernet Sauvignon   **£4.65**
Healthy, clingy, picnic red with grippy black fruit and juicy liveliness.

🍷 9 Morrisons Beaujolais 2010   **£4.69**
Lively, juicy, squashed-raspberry Beaujolais from a brilliant vintage with a tinge of white pepper; it will run out soon.

RED WINES

FRANCE

8 Château Tour de Buch 2009 £6.79
Solid purple colour and 14% alcohol remind what a ripe vintage 2009 was in Bordeaux, making this clean, pure-fruit Merlot-dominated wine memorably generous and forward.

8 Morrisons Claret Bordeaux £6.79
A non-vintage wine, but rounded and developed, with vigorous blackberry fruit.

8 Castelmaures Corbières 2008 £6.99
Gripping, dark and spicy Mediterranean red has a hint of silk; easy, rounded and 14% alcohol.

8 Cuvée Briot Rouge 2009 £7.99
Friendly, straight, brambly Bordeaux 70/30 Merlot/Cabernet mix from great vintage is juicy and wholesome.

8 Morrisons Italian Chianti 2009 £5.39
I promise it does say Italian Chianti on the label, and I was charmed by the cherry perfume, grippy dark fruit with nutty richness, and dry finish. Proper Italian Chianti indeed.

ITALY

8 Italia Primitivo 2010 £7.19
An engaging Puglian varietal with firm but juicy and direct black fruit; ignore discouraging minimalist label.

9 Morrisons The Best Montepulciano
d'Abruzzo 2009 £7.19
Dark, dense and juicy with long, brambly fruit and a defining dry finish, this is healthy, vigorous and very Italian.

RED WINES

ITALY

8 **Morrisons The Best Valpolicella Ripasso 2009** **£7.19**

Nice fruitcake aroma off this quirky Verona wine with dense colour and a dark, pruny-liquorice centre to the intense flavours.

9 **Trezanti Rosso 2010** **£7.99**

Lovely silky rounded surprise Salento (Puglia) red from Negroamaro grapes with mild oak richness, long fruit and spicy highlights.

8 **Barolo Cantine Gemma 2005** **£14.79**

Old wine browning nicely has an authentic, faintly spirity, cold-tea nose and warm, gently spicy cherry fruit with 14% alcohol. Sounds frightful, I realise, but good of its kind.

SOUTH AFRICA

8 **Morrisons South African Shiraz 2010** **£6.39**

There seems more of the Cape than of Shiraz in this tarry, mega-ripe, liquorice-centred, 14% alcohol, oaked fruit bomb, but I like it.

8 **Morrisons The Best Coastal Region Pinotage 2010** **£7.99**

Sinewy-savoury dark fruit in this authentic oaked Pinotage with spiky highlights; assertive, not overweight, and 14% alcohol.

9 **Vergelegen Cabernet Sauvignon Merlot 2008** **£10.39**

Sublime Bordeaux-style wine from top Cape winery is plummy and silky with chocolate, coffee and cedar insinuations and 14.5% alcohol. A safe investment for a grand occasion.

RED WINES

SPAIN

🍷 8 **Morrisons Viña Eneldo Rioja Crianza 2007 £7.99**
Quite light in colour and weight (as plenty of Riojas are), this still has a friendly plumpness of summer soft fruit and a twang of citrus to balance the vanilla oak.

🍷 8 **Morrisons Rioja Reserva 2006** £9.49
Colour is gently browning with age and the sweet creamy oak is catching up with the soft blackcurrant fruit.

WHITE WINES

AUSTRALIA

🍷 8 **Morrisons Australian Chardonnay** £4.69
Non-vintage, but from the redoubtable Kingston Estate in Riverland, this lively unoaked dry white delivers good fruit and zest for the money.

CHILE

🍷 8 **Morrisons The Best Casablanca Valley Chardonnay 2010** £7.99
Spring greens and mango team up equably in this substantial dry white.

FRANCE

🍷 8 **Morrisons French Chardonnay** £4.65
Non-vintage Languedoc is in the soft-ripe apple/touch of buttery scrambled egg style, and really rather good.

🍷 8 **Morrisons French Muscadet 2011** £4.85
Twangy Loire mussel-partner is briny and fresh, with manageable acidity.

🍷 9 **Morrisons Mâcon Villages 2009** £7.15
Gold colour, peachy-tropical Chardonnay aroma and long, rich (but unoaked) fruit should be holding up.

WHITE WINES

9 **Morrisons Petit Chablis 2009** £7.99
Loved this instantly recognisable light-but-firm Chablis with its green-gold colour, flinty Chardonnay whiff and long, mineral flavours. Price is very fair for this sort of quality.

8 **Morrisons Touraine Sauvignon 2011** £7.99
Brisk, generic Loire, much pricier than previous excellent vintage, has lots of asparagus and grassy-briny flavour.

10 **Morrisons The Best Chablis 2009** £10.19
From the same source as the Petit Chablis above, the Union des Viticulteurs, this is a fuller, weightier wine with similar charms. Pure and flinty in the proper Chablis way, it is healthily leesy and long, and – I am told by Marc Vachet of the Viticulteurs – will keep and improve in the bottle for years.

8 **Morrisons Mosel Riesling 2010** £7.19
Soft, apple-fresh and tangy-edged, with 8.5% alcohol.

8 **Morrisons The Best Auslese 2010** £8.99
Balanced Mosel Riesling has ripe appeal and 8% alcohol.

8 **Morrisons Italian Pinot Grigio** £4.65
Likeable non-vintage, well-coloured, peachy-nosed Veneto PG has fresh flavours and a hint of the exotic.

8 **Morrisons Orvieto Classico 2011** £4.99
The delicate Orvieto wines of Umbria are lately out of vogue, but here is a fine reintroduction, fresh with almondy notes and finishing with a clean lemon tang.

WHITE WINES

ITALY

8 **Morrisons Verdicchio Classico 2010**   £4.99
In the kind of amphora-shaped bottle I had believed extinct, a sunny example of the Marches café white with lively, herbaceous, white-fruit charm.

8 **Morrisons The Best Gavi 2011**   £8.19
Lively and long, herbaceous-blanched-hazelnut, discreetly rich, dry Piedmont wine by reliable Araldica.

NEW ZEALAND

8 **Morrisons The Best Marlborough
Sauvignon Blanc 2011**   £7.99
Crisp, nettly and fresh with edgy acidity, this finishes very trim.

8 **Crux Marlborough Sauvignon Blanc 2011**   £10.99
Asparagus on the way in, seagrass and nettles in the glittery green fruit, and fun on the finish.

SPARKLING WINE

FRANCE

8 **Morrisons Champagne Brut**   £19.99
Generous yeasty mouthfiller with lots of Pinot Meunier is good fun and good value.

Sainsbury's

 I first tasted wine from Sainsbury's long ago when the magazine company I worked for happened to have its offices next door to Sainsbury's HQ. I wasn't writing about wine back then, but I have never forgotten that tasting: it was the launch, in effect, of the concept of supermarket own-label wine.

Yes, Sainsbury's invented it. And more than 30 years later, they're still out in front. The Taste the Difference range, launched in 2006, offers truly remarkable diversity and consistency of quality, and its reach extends every year.

Particular strengths are classic-region French red wines from the outstanding 2009 and 2010 vintages, and some cracking whites from 2011. The grand and expensive red wines from Italy, including some from the recently reintroduced 'Classic Selection' range, are very convincing. And I was almost equally taken with a couple of amazingly cheap reds from the bargain-price 'House' wine range introduced with economic perspicacity a couple of years back.

Sainsbury's this year comes out top for maximum-scoring wines, eight all told, and this accurately reflects the standard of both branded and own-label wines that this retailer so reassuringly offers.

Sainsbury's

RED WINES

ARGENTINA

9 Taste the Difference Fairtrade Morador
Malbec 2010   £7.99
Well-adjusted, darkly charming, roast-beef red from
recently recognised Luján de Cuyo region has macho
leather aroma, pruny intensity and real suppleness,
complete with 14.5% alcohol.

8 Viñalba Reserva Cabernet Sauvignon
Malbec Merlot 2010   £9.99
Berry-sweet core to this bumper (14.5% alcohol) grippy
Mendoza blend extends out through juicy fruitiness to a
clean, lipsmacking finish.

AUSTRALIA

8 Taste the Difference Barossa Shiraz 2010   £9.49
Minty monster has artfully contrived balance of cleanly
breaking acidity after the whack of dark, dense, savoury
fruit; 14.5% alcohol.

10 Gulf Station Pinot Noir 2010   £11.99
De Bortoli in the Yarra Valley make this wine in what I
take to be the burgundian manner. It has a lovely limpid
colour, billowing strawberry-cherry nose and complete,
silky, classic discreetly oaked Pinot fruit. Perfect, and half
the price of some burgundian counterparts I can think of.

CHILE

8 Taste the Difference Chilean Merlot 2011   £6.99
Big tarry-ripe food red with black-cherry richness and a
clean clench of tannin; needs meat.

9 Cono Sur Reserva Cabernet Sauvignon 2009 £7.99
Toasty ripeness wraps a long, sweetly seductive, creamily
oaked blackcurrant fruit with ideal weight and 14%
alcohol. Keen price.

RED WINES

FRANCE

9 Longue-Dog Red 2011 £5.49

Jokey take is a seriously good buy nonetheless. Dark maroon, big, friendly brambly style (14% alcohol) of long, juicy-savoury fruit. Rare bargain among popular brands. Deserves a pat.

8 Sainsbury's SO Organic Shiraz 2011 £5.99

Soupy Vin de Pays d'Oc could be mistaken for Aussie (and not just on account of the 'Shiraz' misnomer), but has a brisk Mediterranean edge.

9 Taste the Difference Beaujolais Villages 2009 £6.99

Standout wine is crunchy and bright with raspberry fruit, and demonstrates the staying power of the fabled 2009 Beaujolais vintage.

10 Taste the Difference Faugères 2010 £7.99

I'm top-scoring this because of its typicity. It is every inch a Faugères, from a rather remote outpost in the Languedoc, a refined and poised Grenache/Syrah/Mourvèdre of dark, spicy-savoury grippiness and 14% alcohol.

8 Georges Duboeuf Fleurie 2010 £8.99

Full, ripe and sunny Beaujolais *cru* not as ludicrously overpriced as usual.

8 Taste the Difference Crozes Hermitage 2010 £9.49

Green leafy nose on this pure Syrah from the northern Rhône leads into blueberry fruit already rounding out. It stands out for interest and value.

RED WINES

8 **Château Barreyres 2009** £11.49
Haut-Médoc *cru bourgeois* has proper tobacco-cedar-cassis nose and very ripened (but not cooked) fruit to make an authentic, eager, complete and assertive claret already drinking well.

10 **Taste the Difference Châteauneuf
du Pape 2010** £14.99
I've been waiting years for a supermarket Châteauneuf worthy of the name, and here it is. Colour is already turning and it feels more aged than its years, with the complexity of toasty-juicy-savoury fruits that are the famed village's hallmark. Price is very fair indeed.

8 **Antonin Rodet Pommard 2009** £25.99
Grand burgundy from the 'Classic Selection' has the sort of elegant gravitas you might expect for the money; poised strawberry with a lemon zest, long and slinky classic Pinot Noir.

8 **Barone Ricasoli Rocca Guicciarda
Riserva Chianti Classico 2009** £16.99
I am completely taken in by this near-austere Chianti with its beautiful label and explosive cherry-briar fruit. From the 'Classic Selection'.

9 **Serre Alte Barolo Riserva 2004** £21.99
Dark and browning, this is Barolo with body – an unusual find in a supermarket (it's from the 'Classic Selection') and a special one, with epic ripeness and length, coffee and roses in the fruit and persistent tannin at the finish. Top wine, at a price.

FRANCE

ITALY

Sainsbury's

RED WINES

ITALY

10 Torre de Mastio Amarone della Valpolicella Classico 2008 £22.99

Maybe I need to get out more, but I believe this is the best Amarone I have tasted. It's a fruit cake in a bottle, complete with marzipan, pitch dark with poised intensity (15% alcohol), and quite dry ('amarone' translates as 'bitter'). Guzzle it with hard cheese.

N. ZEALAND

8 Taste the Difference Central Otago Pinot Noir 2010 £9.99

Did I really detect olives on the nose? A delicate Pinot by Kiwi standards, cherry-ripe, discreetly oaked, arguably feminine in character.

PORTUGAL

9 Taste the Difference Douro 2010 £8.99

Porty nose and tight-but-broad-flavoured table wine from the port country made by excellent Quinta do Crasto has rich blackcurrant strands and silkily integrated dark flavours. It's 14% alcohol, deeply satisfying and, amazingly, unoaked.

ROMANIA

10 House Pinot Noir £4.49

Bouncy, non-vintage, Beaujolais-weight Carpathian juice bomb has true Pinot raspberry-earthy vigour, and if memory serves is even more delightful than the one I tasted a year ago and scored 9. So, top marks to this bargain, which has risen in price by just 20p.

S. AFRICA

9 Taste the Difference South African Pinotage 2011 £7.99

I admit I do very often find Cape Pinotages aggressive and sweaty, but this one is cool and refined; lush blueberry fruit with an ideal weight (though 14.5% alcohol) and a sense of fresh vitality. It's big, but not bruising.

RED WINES

SPAIN

8 **Spanish Steps Toro 2011** £6.99
Blood-red monster is a spicy and slick Tempranillo with
minty relish; a great match for big-flavoured fish dishes.

8 **Taste the Difference Priorat 2009** £10.49
I'm always curious to try Priorat, Spain's emerging star
region. This Syrah/Grenache/Carignan blend grips the
tastebuds with a firm, liquorous, black fruit in a velvet
glove, with notes of nutmeg, cinnamon and other more
mysterious spices.

PINK WINES

ENGLAND

7 **Denbies Rose Hill Rosé** £8.99
Novelty non-vintage Surrey pink has cheery magenta
colour and sweetish fruit resembling Pinot Noir though
made from Dornfelder grapes, and 11% alcohol. Decent
effort, but not cheap.

FRANCE

8 **Sainsbury's Cuvée Prestige Côtes du Rhône
Rosé 2011** £5.49
Magenta with bold briar fruit, this is fresh, friendly and
familiar.

8 **Taste the Difference Bordeaux Rosé 2011** £7.99
Dry but by no means ascetic Merlot-based blend has a
pretty salmon colour and fresh cherry-bramble fruit that
lingers nicely.

8 **Taste the Difference Côtes de Provence
Rosé 2011** £7.99
Attractive onion-skin colour translates into a cool, floral
nose and generous, sunny, firm, dry fruit.

WHITE WINES

8 **Taste the Difference Redbridge Creek
Chardonnay 2011** £6.99

Everyday Riverina made by De Bortoli has noticeable apple purity and discreet oak richness.

8 **Leasingham Magnus Riesling 2009** £8.99

Stern, limey Clare Valley wine in the proper mineral manner is perfect for Asian meals, and also with olives.

8 **Bootstraps Chardonnay 2010** £9.99

Sipping this Eden Valley wine is like biting into a thick-skinned Braeburn apple, it's so crisp and grippy, yet it has a yielding richness too (and 14.5% alcohol).

9 **D'Arenberg The Hermit Crab Marsanne
Viognier 2010** £9.99

Another luscious vintage for this perennial McLaren Vale favourite.

8 **Taste the Difference Hunter Valley
Aged Semillon 2006** £9.99

Richly coloured dry wine is zingy with the pineapple and melon style of the Semillon grape (usually a sweet-wine ingredient), and just 10.5% alcohol.

8 **Castillo de Molina Sauvignon Blanc 2011** £8.99

Marked asparagus character to this brightly crisp Elqui Valley dry wine.

8 **Sainsbury's Vin de Pays des Côtes
de Gascogne** £4.49

Non-vintage Colombard makes a fresh and lemony party dry white at a very keen price.

WHITE WINES

8 Sainsbury's Anjou Blanc   **£4.99**
Soft-centred yet tangy non-vintage Loire Chenin Blanc has modest 11.5% alcohol.

8 Les Jardiniers Sauvignon Blanc 2011   **£6.49**
A humble Loire Vin de Pays, this nevertheless has attention-grabbing asparagus savour and lots of crisp freshness.

**8 Taste the Difference Bourgogne
Aligoté 2011**   **£6.99**
Nice mineral example of the only white burgundy not made with Chardonnay, this is mineral rather in the Loire style, and a legitimate conversation piece.

8 Taste the Difference Mâcon Villages 2011   **£6.99**
Sherbet nose and a hint of pétillance in this apple-zesty dry southern burgundy from a difficult vintage.

**9 Taste the Difference Muscadet Sèvre et
Maine Sur Lie 2011**   **£6.99**
Really well-made example of the classic Loire bone-dry white has heaps of briny fruit and unmistakable Muscadet green-fruit tang.

8 Vouvray La Couronne des Plantagenets 2010 **£6.99**
Dry, brisk, even lemony Loire wine has a sunny-ripe sweet middle and just 11.5% alcohol; a natch match for roast chicken lunch.

8 Elegant Frog Viognier 2011   **£8.49**
Once you're past the cliché of the label, this Languedoc dry white is a fine contrivance of de luxe, ripe peach-pear fruit with genuine charm.

WHITE WINES

8 **Taste the Difference Bordeaux**
Sauvignon Blanc 2011 £8.99
Elegant but generous dry white, very much in the
Bordeaux style – a more restrained wine than its New
Zealand counterparts, but equally likeable.

10 **Taste the Difference Languedoc Blanc 2011** £8.99
A lush fruit-basket of flavours makes this bright, fresh,
Mediterranean blend taste a lot more exciting than its
anonymous provenance might promise. A fabulous wine
I fear might get overlooked.

10 **Taste the Difference Pouilly Fumé 2010** £12.79
Still on shelf from last year, when I scored it 10. This
grand Loire Sauvignon is still gorgeous, with a note of
spearmint added to the nose and the sherbet zest lingering
in the long, grassy-asparagus fruit.

9 **Sancerre Roc L'Abbaye 2011** £15.99
Top-of-the range wine from the 'Classic Selection' is a
textbook flinty-grassy Sauvignon with long, long flavours.
Special.

9 **Demoiselles de Larrivet Haut-Brion**
Blanc 2010 £21.99
Millionaire's dry white Bordeaux from the 'Classic
Selection' is a traditional Sauvignon/Semillon blend with
a rush of sleek, lush fruit and a lick of richness from new
oak. Very ripe and 14% alcohol.

8 **Dr L Riesling 2011** £7.39
In a curious blue bottle, a delicious honey-ripe, zippingly
fresh Mosel at just 8.5% alcohol.

WHITE WINES

8 **Taste the Difference Verdicchio Classico
dei Castelli di Jesi 2011** £6.99
Remarkably lively, crisp, dry refresher from the province
of Ancona in central Italy.

8 **Taste the Difference Coolwater Bay
Sauvignon Blanc 2011** £8.49
Asparagus to the fore in this eager, grassy Wairau Valley
item, with attractive heft.

8 **Taste the Difference Awatere Riesling 2011** £9.99
Tangy, stony-fresh, dry match for tricky dishes like salad,
grilled fish and creamy pasta; 11.5% alcohol.

9 **The Ned Pinot Grigio 2011** £9.99
You can buy this splendidly named Waihopai Valley wine
everywhere – and a good thing too. It has the faintest
pink in the colour from skin contact, and a smoky, exotic
Alsace style, without that region's troublesome sugar
levels. A super food wine.

9 **Taste the Difference Albariño 2011** £7.99
There is a deliciously green edge to the lush grassy fruit in
this perennial favourite from Rias Baixas; a superb new
vintage.

8 **Taste the Difference Viñedos Barrihuelo
Rioja Blanco 2011** £8.99
Not much white Rioja around these days, but here's one
to seek out; it's warmly ripe but lemony fresh too, in the
modern style.

SPARKLING WINES

FRANCE

🍷 **10** Sainsbury's Blanc de Noirs Champagne
Brut   £20.99
A perennial top scorer in this guide, this remains my favourite supermarket own-brand champagne, with alluring digestive-biscuit nose, creamy, long fruit and a reassuring feeling of bottle-age.

🍷 **9** Sainsbury's Blanc de Blancs Champagne
Brut   £22.49
The score is conditional upon this crisp, biscuity, generous and very evidently Chardonnay sparkler being on discount (around £15), which it seems perpetually to be.

ITALY

🍷 **7** Torretta di Mondelli Prosecco Spumante   £10.49
Dry with a caramel centre, this Veneto fizz does have some white-fruit flavour, and 11% alcohol.

N. ZEALAND

🍷 **7** Taste the Difference Lightly Sparkling
Sauvignon Blanc 2011   £11.99
If you like a fresh, crisp, gently frothy sparkler and you like Sauvignon, you will like this.

Tesco

 Although Tesco as a business is said to be as big as its nearest two rivals, Asda and Sainsbury's, put together, this grocery Goliath is said to be losing market share and slowing down in profitability.

I saw no symptoms of this alleged malaise at this year's giant Tesco wine tasting. The large team of buyers, winemakers and 'product development managers' who are always on hand looked pretty confident to me.

They have reason to be so, because the wines are as good as ever. And they are more diverse. The range might have been tightened up, but the casualties seem to be wines they can well do without.

I came away with the feeling that Europe is fighting back very effectively in the battle to find space on the shelves of Britain's biggest licensed retailer. The boring megabrands from the southern hemisphere look poor value against Tesco's ever-expanding Finest range of own-labels, most of which I am glad to see are sourced in France, Italy and Spain.

Do look at Tesco's wine website. There are always discounts galore, many of them on wines not on promotion in the stores. The minimum order is just one six-bottle case and you get free delivery if ordering more than £99 worth of wine. And the delivery, which I have tested myself on more than one occasion, is formidably efficient. Order before noon one day, and you'll get your wine the next.

RED WINES

ARGENTINA

8 La Mascota Malbec 2009 £11.00
Grand, dark, savoury, leather-scented, richly ripe meat matcher. By the case online only.

8 Tim Adams Protégé Tempranillo 2009 £11.00
Nicely defined black-fruit Tempranillo has healthy weight and tidy finish; 14% alcohol. By the case online only.

AUSTRALIA

9 The Lioness Pinot Noir 2010 £12.99
Aussie Pinot is definitely on the up. This has a lovely limpid ruby colour, pale but glowing, and the earthy soft-fruit nose is succeeded by poised, perfectly ripe fruit with ideal trim and 14% alcohol.

8 Penfolds Bin 128 2010 £14.49
Grenache, Shiraz and Mourvèdre Barossa blend in a roasty-dark northern Rhône style, warming, savoury and 14.5% alcohol. Fine Wine stores.

**8 Pikes and Joyce Adelaide Hills
Pinot Noir 2008** £17.99
Orange-brown, defined and stimulatingly, bright, earthy Pinot of real charm and 14% alcohol. Fine Wine stores.

CHILE

8 Marques de Casa Concha Syrah 2008 £11.99
Savoury grilled darkness to the edge of this dignified spicy oaked wine from Concha y Toro; note 15% alcohol.

**8 Viña Chocolan Cabernet Franc
Reserve 2010** £11.99
This might not be for everybody, but I loved the leafy Cabernet Franc greenness amid the slinky, ripe, classically Chilean charm; it has a fine grip at the finish to make it a great steak matcher; 14.5% alcohol.

RED WINES

FRANCE

9 Tesco Simply Côtes du Rhône 2011 £3.79
Simple indeed, but a deliciously raspy and fresh, light but firmly fruity, typical CdR at an incomprehensible price.

8 Tesco Simply Malbec 2011 £4.99
Part Cahors, part Minervois, a nice dark and plummy chewy red with a roasty centre. Barbecue wine.

8 Finest Côtes Catalanes Carignan 2011 £6.99
Hedgerow-fruit liveliness in this bouncingly warm, sweet-centred southern red.

8 Finest Plan de Dieu 2011 £6.99
Plump, peppery Côtes du Rhône Villages is ripe and substantial (14% alcohol) and a nice easy weight.

10 Finest Côtes Catalanes Grenache 2010 £7.79
I keep coming back to this wine; it is vigorously brambly and yet smoothly integrated, long, richly spicy and full of promise. Seems to be rounding out with age; this vintage featured here last year, so buy now while it lasts – it is regularly on discount online.

10 Juliénas Duboeuf 2010 £8.99
Absolutely spot-on purple strawberry-raspberry Beaujolais *cru* of – dare I say it – feminine suppleness and balancing crunchy freshness and crispness at the edge of the fruit.

**8 Finest Château Fonguillon Montagne
St Emilion 2009** £9.79
Proper Merlot-based St Emilion satellite with elegant cedary-blackberry fruit and savoury tannin from a famously ripe (14% alcohol) Bordeaux vintage.

RED WINES

FRANCE

8 **Finest Crozes Hermitage 2009** £9.99
The only affordable northern Rhône appellation in a perfect vintage produced this rarely ripe blueberry-fruit pure Syrah red of utterly distinctive character.

8 **Savigny les Beaune Premier Cru Aux Clous 2008** £18.79
Legendary Nicolas Potel made this elegant and emphatically ripe burgundy, now in its prime. Fine Wine stores.

9 **Château Brown 2006** £21.79
In a line-up of posh clarets from Tesco's Fine Wine range this Pessac Cabernet/Merlot stood out; healthy, natural-tasting, vivid maturing wine of proper poise.

ITALY

9 **Finest Teroldego Vigneti Delle Dolomiti 2010** £7.99
Worthy successor to the 2009 vintage of this bold new wine from subalpine Italy, it's darkly fresh and minty, with leafy cool-climate purity of defined redcurrant fruit. Price is up by £2, sadly.

9 **Gran Conti Rosso del Molise Riserva 2008** £8.99
Dark Adriatic red blended from an odd mixture of Montepulciano and Aglianico grapes contrives to be both cushiony and muscular; also truffly, strawberry-sweet, spicy and rich. Look out for it on regular discount.

RED WINES

10 Squinzano Monte Nobile Rosso Riserva 2008 £9.99

Another superb vintage for this perpetual favourite from Puglia. Dark, ripe and reassuring with cherry-chocolate nuance and a toasty richness, Squinzano (it brings on a smile just to say the name) is as perpetually on cut-price offer, especially online, as it is perpetually delicious.

8 Santa Cristina Chianti Superiore 2010 £10.99

Elegantly austere Chianti by Antinori has a leafy quality to the classic intense-cherry middle fruit and crisp finish.

9 Villa Antinori Rosso Toscano 2008 £15.79

From the Chianti dynasty of Antinori, this isn't Chianti because besides 55% Sangiovese (the Chianti grape) it comprises Cabernet, Merlot and Syrah too. It's gorgeous, the cat's whiskers rather than a dog's dinner. Fine Wine stores.

8 Brunello di Montalcino Rendola 2004 £20.29

I am continually disappointed by Brunello but this hits the spot; browning colour, maturing, rather than decaying, Chianti-de-luxe fruit with coffee pungency and cherry-sweet lushness. Fine Wine stores.

8 Felsina Berardenga Chianti Classico 2008 £20.29

Into each life a little truly beautiful Chianti Classico should pour. Silky but rugged-abrasive, cherry-gamey maturing wine with proper nutskin finish. Fine Wine stores.

Red Wines

Tesco

N. Zealand

8 **Finest Central Otago Pinot Noir 2010** £9.99
Subtle and restrained by usual Kiwi standards, a beguiling minty-strawberry Pinot of cool elegance; tight-knit, though, and very likeable.

Portugal

8 **Finest Touriga Nacional 2011** £7.79
Opaque maroon Alentejo wine from the great grape of the Douro has a porty nose and cassis richness, but comes out dry and brisk. Try with roast lamb.

S. Africa

8 **Bellingham Bernard Series Syrah 2010** £10.99
Neatly defined flavours in a soupy whole; I couldn't help liking this spicy, distinctive, 14% alcohol wine.

8 **Gran Tesoro Garnacha 2011** £4.29
Consistently cheap and cheerful juicy kitchen red to drink young. Don't keep this wine too long. I held over a few 2009s, but the wine died in the bottle.

9 **Finest Old Vines Garnacha 2010** £7.79
From Campo de Borja, a truly gripping and intense rich cassis-and-spice fruit bomb with tight, dry finish and 14% alcohol. Needs grilled meat or strong cheese.

Spain

10 **Finest Viña Mara Rioja Reserva 2007** £9.49
I have trouble keeping up with changing vintages and designations of these Viña Maras, made for Tesco by Baron de Ley, but this one jumps out with its seductive vanilla and raspberry-essence nose, and fruit to match; lovely weight, and a thrill to drink.

RED WINES

SPAIN

 7 Finest Viña Mara Rioja Gran
Reserva 2004 £13.79

Browning colour, fruit not (quite) drying out in this genteel old thing; I much prefer the Reserva 2007.

USA

 8 Ravenswood Lodi Old Vine
Zinfandel 2009 £9.99

The puzzling appeal of Zinfandel is partially explained by this bright, berry-fruit spicy oaked blend (with Petite Sirah); it has persuasive abrasion, crisp acidity and 14.5% alcohol. Try with roast duck or a bacon sandwich.

PINK WINES

FRANCE

 7 Finest Domaine de Sours Rosé 2011 £7.99

Shell-pink and packed with berry fruit, a Bordeaux wine with a strongly blackcurranty character, finishing dry.

PORTUGAL

 7 Finest Touriga Nacional Rosé 2011 £6.99

Big Alentejo pink from the main port grape has quite a lot of residual sugar (just like port), but it works; a food wine that would suit salads.

SPAIN

 8 Gran Tesoro Garnacha Rosé 2011 £3.49

Magenta, with a medicinal nose, this is a sweetish party pink of shameless allure.

 7 Finest Navarra Rosé 2011 £6.99

Shocking pink with a lot of cheerfully assertive Garnacha fruit; an outdoor wine just shy of dry.

WHITE WINES

AUSTRALIA

8 Finest Boranup Sauvignon Semillon 2011 £9.99
A crisply dry white from a grape blend better known for
sweet wines, this has a relishable tropical-grassy balance
of flavours.

8 Finest Denman Semillon 2011 £9.99
Pineapple richness in a crisp, dry medium makes this
Hunter Valley freshener highly distinctive and enjoyable;
11% alcohol.

8 Finest Tingleup Riesling 2011 £9.99
I cannot resist this perennially quirky dry wine; it's a
long, mineral, limey food-matching Riesling in a very
Australian tradition. Poultry, Asian, salads.

8 Jacob's Creek Steingarten Riesling 2011 £16.29
Sweet, grapey nose but a dry, racy-appley wine with
discreet limey acidity and a lot of convincing varietal
character. Fine Wine stores.

CHILE

9 Emiliana O Viognier 2011 £7.99
It's a great year for Viognier. This is rich with the
trademark preserved-fruit savour, apricot included, but
also full of white-fruit freshness, with a poised tangy
finish; 14% alcohol. Only in biggest 87 stores or online.

**9 Marques de Casa Concha
Chardonnay 2009** £11.99
Lush oaked Limari wine in the Meursault tradition is a
lot better than mere pastiche. From Concha y Toro, a
warning shot to the Burgundians; 14% alcohol.

WHITE WINES

8 Cono Sur 20 Barrels Sauvignon Blanc 2010 £13.99

Spritzy-fresh Casablanca Sauvignon might look pricy for Chile but it is exceptionally well-made and crisply defined. Special.

6 JP Chenet Light Colombard Chardonnay 2011 £4.99

Reduced-alcohol (5.5%) wine from the brand known for its wonky bottles, though this bottle seemed less wonky (more sober?). An OK off-dry white if you must drink this sort of thing, as countless Tesco customers apparently do.

7 Tesco Mâcon Villages Blanc 2011 £4.99

Inexpensive for burgundy, this has a sweet spearmint nose, sunny sweet-apple fruit and retreating acidity. Mild-mannered.

8 Tesco White Burgundy 2010 £6.79

Lush and vivid unoaked white is keen and fresh, illustrating the lasting powers of the excellent 2010 vintage.

8 Finest Saint Mont 2010 £6.99

Inviting sweet nutty nose and rich colour to this generous, sunny-ripe autumn-fruit, dry and thought-provoking Pyrenean wine.

9 Finest Côtes de Gascogne 2011 £7.29

From a terrific range of 'Finest Côtes' wines at Tesco, this richly coloured dry white has buckets of exotic, deep-south ripe orchard fruit from Gros Manseng with a lick of Sauvignon.

WHITE WINES

10 Finest Picpoul de Pinet 2011 £7.29
Worthy successor to shining 2010 vintage, this has lots of colour, zingy aroma, and lashings of tangy-breezy white fruit. Currently rather a trendy wine, but deservedly so, this also scores for presentation in its quirky bottle.

8 Mmm Sauvignon Blanc 2010 £12.00
Generic Loire wine by distinguished Fournier estate could easily be AC Sancerre; it is stony-fresh and burgeoning with gooseberry-nettle fruit. Online only.

8 Blason de Bourgogne Pouilly Fuissé 2010 £13.79
Swish Mâconnais has near-eggy richness of peachy Chardonnay fruit and pronounced minerality; so well-made.

8 Domaine de Bel Air Pouilly Fumé
Cuvée des Acoins 2011 £14.99
Flinty, pure-fruit Loire Sauvignon lives up to the elevated name of its appellation.

8 Trimbach Alsace Gewürztraminer
Réserve 2005 £17.99
Long-aged but still very perky and plushly ripe, lychee-laden Gewürz from a grand producer has nifty balance; in a different league from the standard stuff – at a price. Fine Wine stores.

8 Le Cellier des Princes Châteauneuf du
Pape Blanc 2010 £20.00
You don't see much white Châteauneuf in the supermarkets, but fans of the luscious oaked white-fruit style of this rarity should like this one. By the case online only.

WHITE WINES

ITALY

🍷 **7** **Simply Soave Classico 2011**   £4.49
Price is close to its principal attraction, but it does have the right almondy richness amid the dry, near-green fruit.

🍷 **8** **Finest Falanghina 2011**   £5.99
Aromatic dry white from Puglia has white orchard fruit with a convincing citrus edge. Seafood pasta would be a fine match.

🍷 **8** **Finest Pinot Grigio Trentino 2011**   £6.99
Cool-climate mountain wine translates into stony-fresh flavours; a sharpener among PGs.

🍷 **9** **Finest Soave Classico Superiore 2010**   £6.99
Immediately likeable Verona dry white has generous colour and nutty-tangy perfume, richness and weight of body, and a lemony edge. Very good value for this quality.

NEW ZEALAND

🍷 **6** **First Cape Light Sauvignon Blanc**   £4.49
If you must drink reduced-alcohol wine, this curiosity with lots of residual sugar and added acidity (and 5.5% alcohol) might as well do.

🍷 **8** **Ara Pathway Sauvignon Blanc 2011**   £8.99
Bracing Marlborough grassy white will take a firm hold of your tastebuds.

🍷 **9** **Finest Marlborough Chardonnay 2010**   £9.99
Yellow-gold colour and extravagantly rich, oak-creamed fruit in this huge wine are counterbalanced by a brisk minerality that is quintessentially Kiwi. Made by redoubtable Wither Hills, with 14% alcohol.

WHITE WINES

NEW ZEALAND

🍷 **8** **Kim Crawford Marlborough**
Sauvignon Blanc 2011 **£11.79**
Spectacularly zingy sea-bright Sauvignon has long, grassy lushness. Fine Wine stores.

🍷 **9** **Cloudy Bay Chardonnay 2008** **£19.79**
What's in a name? This icon lives up to it: huge colour, exciting creamy-coconut sweet-apple aroma, luscious long, mineral fruit, very ripe (14% alcohol) but tightly defined, too. I fell for it completely. Fine Wine stores.

S. AFRICA

🍷 **10** **Finest Swartland Chenin Blanc 2011** **£6.99**
'Butch, even brusque', I noted of this eagerly dry and keen palate freshener, which also happens to have a lot of 'honey and peach' richness in its fruit. Intrigued? Do try it. I think it's the best Cape white around this price I have tasted.

SPAIN

🍷 **8** **Finest Palomino 2011** **£7.29**
Made by sherry bodega Barbadillo from the sherry grape Palomino Fino, this has a ghost of bone-dry pale sherry in it: a crisp, tangy refresher.

🍷 **8** **Finest Palestra Rueda 2011** **£7.79**
Seagrass and white-peach ripeness marry charmingly in this finely poised dry white from the elusive Verdejo grape.

SPARKLING WINES

8 **Broadwood's Folly Brut** £16.99
Plausible ripe-but-defined crisp sparkler from Denbies, in Surrey.

ENGLAND

9 **Finest Premier Cru Champagne** £20.99
Now my favourite Tesco own-label champagne, it's 70/30 Chardonnay/Pinot Noir, cohesive and ripely satisfying.

FRANCE

9 **Finest Bisol Prosecco di Valdobbiadene** £9.99
A 'brut' style vigorous fizz with ample orchard fruit and a lemony edge; attractive package, especially at frequent special-offer price nearer £6.

ITALY

FORTIFIED WINE

9 **Finest Manzanilla Sherry 50cl** £5.90
It's bone dry, but jangling with tangy, pungent seaside fruit; a superb manzanilla made by Barbadillo, very much more exciting than its fino counterpart (15% alcohol).

SPAIN

Waitrose

 Waitrose has, by a country mile, the widest selection of wines anywhere. The range, on paper at least, is twice the size on offer at any other supermarket chain. Not even Majestic, the last of the national specialist wine-merchants, competes.

The range has always been enormous, and now the network of stores is starting to catch up with it. Once confined to London and the South East, it's now pretty much nationwide. In not much more than a decade, the branch count has doubled to nearly 250, and most of us now have one within reasonable reach.

It's worth the journey. The choice of wines is deep as well as wide. There are more than 70 different wines from Italy, over 40 from the Rhône Valley, and superb selections from Alsace and the Loire, Germany, Portugal and New Zealand. The sherries, including the own-label Solera Jerezana range, and other fortified wines are legendary.

The prices, I promise, are fair. While a large proportion of the wines are unique to Waitrose, brands also sold by rival supermarkets are clearly priced to compete. Waitrose is sensitive to the notion that its groceries are more expensive than elsewhere, and is currently running an uncharacteristic advertising campaign to assure shoppers that prices for thousands of items exactly match those at Tesco.

Given that Tesco has 30.7 per cent of the market, compared to Waitrose's mere 4.5 per cent, I suppose this is rather impressive. And it doesn't prevent Waitrose from discounting prices. There are always dozens of wines on special offer, and they are mostly genuine bargains.

Not all the wines in the vast range are available in every store, but all can be bought from waitrose.com/wine. You can order any mix you like, which makes Waitrose unique in this respect. Marks & Spencer and Tesco, the only other chains doing wine on the web, do case sales only.

RED WINES

8 **Tilimuqui Fairtrade Cabernet Sauvignon/ Bonarda 2011** £7.19

Nicely toasted richness to this Famatina Valley blend has a liquorice middle and developed fruit. Good balancing red for chilli dishes.

8 **Kaiken Cabernet Sauvignon 2010** £8.49

Sweet but not icky, super-ripe (14.5% alcohol) Mendoza gripper has a polished feel to it.

9 **Catena Malbec 2010** £12.49

Hate the new labels on the iconic Catena wines (definitely Argentine premier league), but still love this defining, dark, sinewy-but-malleable, juicy gripper; 14% alcohol.

8 **Clos de los Siete 2009** £13.99

Mostly Malbec Mendoza of rich, creamy darkness, perfectly pitched for savoury fruit; 14% alcohol.

8 **See Saw Shiraz/Mourvèdre 2010** £8.99

Purple-black blend from both Barossa and Hunter valleys is made with European-style restraint and balance, yet shows Aussie upfrontness too (14% alcohol). It worked on me.

9 **Waitrose Reserve Shiraz 2010** £9.99

Blood-red Barossa made by St Hallett is tanned rather than roasted, savoury, juicy, cushiony and comforting, with 14.5% alcohol. A really successful own-label.

Side labels: ARGENTINA | AUSTRALIA

RED WINES

AUSTRALIA

 8 **Bird in the Hand, Two in the Bush Shiraz 2010** £10.99

I ignored the name and tried it anyway. Glad I did, as it's another ideally balanced Shiraz; sunny-spicy ripeness (14.5% alcohol), with a keen counterpoint of acidity.

CHILE

8 **Viña Leyda Single Vineyard Pinot Noir 2008** £14.99

Big mouthful of plump, ripe fruit with creamy richness and brisk trim, somehow thoroughly Chilean; 14.5% alcohol.

FRANCE

 9 **Cuvée Chasseur 2011** £4.69

Amazingly consistent Waitrose stalwart from Languedoc is brambly and lively but also robust and developed. Top buy at under a fiver.

 8 **Montgravet Cabernet Sauvignon/ Merlot 2011** £4.99

Deep, hearty southern blend is a bargain.

8 **Waitrose Reserve Claret 2011** £5.99

Fresh and healthy young pure-Merlot wine is a safe bet.

8 **Château St Nicolas 2010** £7.99

Spicy, intense-blackberry Roussillon with 14% alcohol is grippy and long.

8 **Laforêt Beaujolais 2011** £7.99

Special Beaujolais from the third auspicious vintage in a row, this has shape as well as joyous juiciness.

RED WINE

9 **Les Nivières Saumur 2010** £7.99
Perennial favourite is bright and supremely fresh in this
sunny vintage; its pleasing leafiness responds very well to
chilling.

8 **Georges Duboeuf Chiroubles 2011** £9.99
Cru Beaujolais has structure and violet perfume above
and beyond the ordinary; a substantial wine that will last.

9 **Domaine de la Croix de Chaintres**
Saumur-Champigny 2010 £10.99
Forcefully fruity Cabernet Franc from Filliatreau, a top
Saumur estate, this has the crunchy-leafy fresh berry style
that typifies, and idealises, red Saumur.

8 **Chorey-Lès-Beaune Joseph Drouhin 2009** £15.99
Fine, earthy-ripe burgundy with creamy-toffee depths
and vivid, silky Pinot fruit.

9 **Givry Domaine Besson Le Haut**
Colombier 2010 £15.99
From the Chalonnais of southern Burgundy, a lovely
wild-cherry Pinot Noir with full, long, intense fruit.

8 **Blason du Rhône Châteauneuf du**
Pape 2010 £20.99
I got a whiff of cappuccino off this big (14.5% alcohol)
multi-layered and ripe oaked de luxe wine, and liked it.

8 **Terso Rosso** £4.79
Dark and deep-south-ripe food red (sticky pasta, oily fish)
from Puglia has a volcanic tinge and is good value.

FRANCE

ITALY

ITALY

🍷 8 **Vignale Valpolicella 2011** £5.49
Sweet strawberry nose and bright matching fruit in this
charming Verona lightweight.

🍷 8 **Umani Ronchi Montepulciano
d'Abruzzo 2011** £5.99
Waitrose perennial seems denser and juicier than of
memory.

🍷 8 **Chianti Poggiotondo Cerro del
Masso 2009** £8.99
A spartan style but Chianti as it should be, with keen-
edged dark berry fruit. Food wine: lamb or beef.

🍷 9 **Bisceglia Gudarra Aglianico del
Vulture 2008** £10.99
Vulture is a Basilicato volcano and you get a whiff of
brimstone amid the spicy perfume; cushiony, plump but
spicy dark fruit; 14% alcohol. Online only.

🍷 8 **Oddero Barolo 2007** £23.99
Show-off's wine, copper in colour, elegant cherries-in-a-
marble-hall perfume and a big, slick, strong fruit with
14.5% alcohol. Safe investment.

N. ZEALAND

🍷 8 **Mountford Estate Village
Pinot Noir 2008** £24.99
Expensive Waipara Valley thriller is rosé pale but firm,
sinuous and seductively ripe (14% alcohol). Online only.

PORTUGAL

🍷 8 **Sogrape Pena de Pato 2009** £8.29
From the once-popular Dão region, a savoury and
distinctive throwback red to bring back happy memories.

RED WINES

PORTUGAL

8 Cortes de Cima Syrah 2010 £11.49
Like a rich blackberry pie, with cream, a lovely luxury
Alentejo red delivering big juicy fruit and 14% alcohol.

ROMANIA

8 La Umbra Merlot 2011 £5.99
Full, ripe black-cherry red is correctly dry and balanced
and likeable.

SOUTH AFRICA

9 Journey's End Shiraz 2007 £15.99
Online only, and to me an unexpected style from the
Stellenbosch, but this is such a perfectly pitched Syrah,
with elegance, juiciness, and gentle spice, that I must give
it space.

9 Thelema Shiraz 2008 £16.99
Another expensive online-only Stellenbosch Syrah
(Shiraz, forsooth), this is a world-class wine of superb
balance and structure; 14.5% alcohol.

SPAIN

8 El Guia Tinto 2011 £3.99
Deep purple, newly squished berry Campo de Borja
glugger is copiously fruity, clean, brisk and cheap.

**8 Rioja Finca Labarca Vendimia Selecciónada
Tempranillo 2010** £7.49
Easy smooth oaked gripper has vivid ripe fruit; healthy
mouthfeel.

9 Viña Fuerte Garnacha 2010 £7.99
New look for this eternal favourite seems to usher in a
more elegant edition of the potent, pruny-spicy gripper
from Calatayud; 14.5% alcohol but rather genteel in its
darkly muscular way.

RED WINES

SPAIN

🍷 8 **Blasón de San Juan Crianza 2009**   £12.99
Ribera del Duero with typical dark, minty, sleek fruit of portentous weight and 14.5% alcohol.

PINK WINES

FRANCE

🍷 8 **Chat-en-Oeuf Rosé 2011**   £5.99
Crisp, fresh, hedgerow Pays d'Oc pink merits the popularity of this jocular brand.

🍷 8 **Domaine de Sainte Rose Coquille d'Oc**
Rosé 2011   £7.29
Shell label, shell-pink colour and a suitably dry Languedoc pink holiday wine to relish with shellfish.

🍷 9 **Mirabeau Provence Rosé 2011**   £8.99
Salmon-pink Syrah/Grenache floral bloom and strawberry-orchard fresh dry fruit in this elegant wine. It tastes pink, and is at the level where rosé starts to be interesting.

🍷 8 **Petit Rimouresque Rosé 2010**   £10.99
Onion-skin-coloured, delicate, floral Côtes de Provence pink from a *cru classé* estate is poised but lush and elegantly fresh.

GREECE

🍷 8 **Phaedra Xynomavro Rosé 2011**   £8.99
Shocking-pink, dry, fresh, strawberry-ripe, Macedonian wine from a region with a climate allegedly similar to that of Bordeaux.

ITALY

🍷 8 **Inycon Growers' Selection Nero d'Avola**
Rosé 2011   £6.99
Party-frock-pink dry Sicilian is generously endowned with fresh, soft, summer fruit.

PINK WINES

SPAIN

🍷 8 **El Guia Rosado 2011** £3.99
Fleshy-but-fresh and dry-finishing magenta cherry pink from Utiel-Requena is cheap but good.

🍷 8 **Marqués de Cáceres Rosado 2011** £8.99
A big, bright, Tempranillo pink from a famous Rioja bodega, this scores for firm, crunchy briar-strawberry fruit and a lipsmacking finish.

WHITE WINES

FRANCE

🍷 8 **Cuvée Pêcheur 2011** £4.69
Ugni Blanc/Colombard blend from Gers might not bode well but this is real fun; nutty-cabbage nose, very fresh and wholesome dry white with 11.5% alcohol.

🍷 8 **Montgravet Chardonnay 2011** £4.99
Of no fixed abode but a smartly packaged, soft-but-defined, apple-fresh cheapie of character.

🍷 8 **Ackerman Chenin Blanc 2011** £5.79
Loire Vin de Pays has honey heart, fresh style and dry finish with 11.5% alcohol; nicely contrived party white.

🍷 8 **Champteloup Muscadet Sèvre et Maine 2011** £5.99
One of a number of exceptional Muscadets I've tasted from 2011, this is bracing without being eyewatering, super-fresh, very dry, with lots of tangy white fruit.

WHITE WINES

9 **Cave de Lugny Mâcon-Villages 2011** £7.49
Miles better than other 2011s I have tried from the same
source, this is a fine, fresh, stony, apple-sweet Chardonnay
from southern Burgundy, with hints of spearmint and
marzipan.

10 **Fief Guérin Muscadet Côtes de Grandlieu
Sur Lie 2011** £7.49
Big-flavoured briny and crisp oyster wine of outstanding
interest. It's not from the usual Sèvre et Maine appellation,
but it's still my favourite Muscadet of the year.

9 **Laurent Miquel Vendanges Nocturnes
Viognier 2011** £8.49
Yet another excellent dry Pays d'Oc Viognier, this time
night-harvested (stops the newly picked grapes cooking
under the Mediterranean sun); ideal luscious-lemon
balance.

8 **Domaine Félines Picpoul de Pinet 2011** £8.99
Well-coloured, leesy-briny, Mediterranean fish matcher.

10 **Domaine de Vieux Vauvert 2011** £8.99
The label designation 'medium-dry' doesn't do this very
delicious Vouvray (Loire) justice; from Chenin Blanc, it's
a tour de force of balance, honeysuckle perfume, luscious
autumn fruit, and brisk, tangy finish (a shade under 12%
alcohol).

8 **Cave de Turckheim Gewürztraminer 2011** £9.49
I am mystified by the Turckheim co-op's monopoly of
UK supermarket Alsace wine; much is dull, but this is a
fresher, less-sugary Gewürz than usual.

WHITE WINES

8 Laurent Miquel l'Atelier Vermentino 2011 £9.99
Herbaceously scented, dry, fresh Pays d'Oc has cool, almondy-orchardy savour typical of Vermentino grape, once exclusive to Sardinia; distinctive.

9 Le Passé Athentique St Mont 2010 £9.99
Exotic Pyrenean dry wine with powerful grapefruit aroma and correspondingly tangy freshness of flavour; plenty of orchard nuance too.

8 Waitrose Chablis 2011 £10.99
Proper Chablis with the right mix of richness and flint, fresh but cerebral and worth the money.

10 Arnaud de Villeneuve Ambré Hors d'Age Rivesaltes 1985 £13.99
Mediterranean *vin doux naturel* more than 25 years old is a revelation: lovely bronze colour, nose an array of sun-dried fruits and blossoms, the weight of the most elegant sherry, a smoky, nutty, wildly fruity just-off-dry aperitif of unique wonder; 15.6% alcohol. Chill it.

9 Château Roquefort Roquefortissime 2009 £13.99
Rich, dry Bordeaux white is pure Sauvignon and pure luxury, lushly ripe with a touch of creamy oak and a lemon twang for perfect balance. Name is very odd.

9 Château Jolys Cuvée Jean Jurançon 2009 £14.49
Fabulous pure-gold ambrosial late-harvested Petit Manseng from esoteric Pyrenean AC of Jurançon is of luscious sweetness but dancing weight.

WHITE WINES

🍷 10 Joseph Drouhin Rully Premier Cru 2010 £14.99

Can't fault this southern burgundy (Chalonnais); perfectly poised between slaking refreshment and luxuriant, leesy, part-new-oaked Chardonnay fruit in perfect nick. It's the ideal expression of the grape.

🍷 8 Philippe Zinck Riesling Eichberg
Grand Cru 2009 £15.99

Exotic, ripe, racy-but-lush Alsace wine is actually reasonably priced for a *grand cru*. Only a few megastores or online.

🍷 9 Château Bastor-Lamontagne
Sauternes 2004 £25.99

Bronze-gold mature Sauternes of great reputation is pure nectar, 14% alcohol and for a full-size bottle, unusually fair in its price. If it has to be Sauternes, this is the best one you'll find in any supermarket. Biggest 85 stores or online.

🍷 8 Kendermann's Special Edition
Pinot Grigio 2011 £6.99

Dependable, smoky, dry Rheinhessen wine with raciness and interest, a huge improvement on the Veneto kind.

🍷 9 Dr Loosen Urziger Würzgarten Riesling
Kabinett 2011 £15.99

Delightful racy Moselle crackles with ripe condition; honeyed-but-zesty, perfectly balanced and fresh, with 7.5% alcohol.

WHITE WINES

GREECE

🍷 8 **Hatzidakis Assyrtiko 2011** £10.99
Bumper (14.5% alcohol) dry, prickly-fresh and
explosively fruity food white (seafood and feta salad,
obviously), from volcanic island of Santorini.

🍷 9 **Vignale Pinot Grigio 2011** £4.99
A cheap Veneto PG that I really, really like, for once. It is
plump and ripe in the Alsace manner, dry but smoky, with
suggestions of honey and grapiness.

🍷 8 **Birgi Grillo 2011** £5.49
Dry, herbaceous, lemon-edged Sicilian refresher is a
characterful bargain.

🍷 8 **Triade Fiano/Falanghina/Greco 2011** £8.99
Campania blend of three interesting grape varieties makes
for an intriguing, fresh, aromatic dry white.

🍷 8 **St Michael-Eppon Gewürztraminer 2010** £12.99
From the Alpine foothills of the Südtirol Alto Adige, an
unmistakable lychee-and-roses Gewürz, but drier and
more pleasantly abrasive than most Alsace counterparts.
Megastores and online.

🍷 8 **Inama Vigneti di Foscarino Soave
Classico 2010** £18.99
Soave cognoscenti (an endangered species, I suspect)
will like this yellow, intense, nutty-lemony, luxuriantly
oxidative specialty wine. Megastores and online.

ITALY

WHITE WINES

8 Cowrie Bay Sauvignon Blanc 2011 £5.99
Everywhere you look there are suddenly cheap Kiwi wines, even in Waitrose. This one has gooseberry freshness and trademark assertive NZ fruit.

8 Jackson Estate Stich Sauvignon Blanc 2011 £12.79
Bracing nettly Marlborough tingler that really makes you sit up; terrifically stimulating.

8 Te Whare Ra TWR Gewürztraminer 2010 £19.99
A riot of aromas and flavours in this super-ripe (14% alcohol), typically lychee/tropical-fruit-salad Gewürz from Marlborough's oldest plantation (1979!); huge fun at a price. Online only.

8 Man O'War Valhalla Chardonnay 2009 £23.99
Pricier than Cloudy Bay and made by a man called McTavish, this is gold in colour, extravagantly oaked, exotic and oxidative in a managed sort of way, with 14.5% alcohol. Online only.

9 Quinta de Azevedo Vinho Verde 2011 £7.49
This seems to get drier and drier vintage by vintage, reverting to the correct vinho verde style, perhaps. Brisk, pétillant refresher of truly distinctive style and just 11% alcohol.

8 Puklavec & Friends Sauvignon Blanc 2011 £8.99
Gooseberry ripe and grassy fresh Sauvignon from the vineyards of Kog, Vinski Vrh and Mali Brebrovnik. What's not to like?

NEW ZEALAND

PORTUGAL

SLOVENIA

WHITE WINES

S. AFRICA

🍷 8 **Vredenhof Cellar Reserve Chardonnay 2011** £6.99
Apples, hazelnuts and comfort, with 14% alcohol, in this discreetly oaked bargain.

🍷 8 **El Guia Blanco 2011** £3.99
Fresh, dry, inoffensive throwing vino de mesa ('table wine') from Galicia.

SPAIN

🍷 8 **Cune Barrel Fermented Rioja 2011** £9.49
Another likeable vintage for this mildly reconstructed white Rioja, vanilla rich and yet briskly fresh, without the oxidation of the old days.

🍷 8 **Taboexa Albariño Rias Baixas 2011** £9.99
Long, white, orchard-fruit and grassy lushness from Galicia.

SPARKLING WINES

ENGLAND

9 Ridgeview Merret Bloomsbury 2009 £22.99
Very good Sussex sparkler from the Champagne cépage
is bready with a fine tiny-bubble mousse and ideal fruit-
freshness balance. This really competes, even in price
terms.

8 Nyetimber Sparkling Rosé 2008 £45.00
You'll need a patriotic thirst to swallow the price, but
this is a beautiful pink fizz from Chardonnay and Pinot
Noir with definition and crispness. From megastores and
online.

FRANCE

**9 Waitrose Brut Special Reserve
Vintage 2004** £29.99
To me, the outstanding champagne among Waitrose's
quite extensive own-label line-up; it's the most expensive,
too. Richly coloured, mellow brioche-nosed, pure-
Chardonnay mature P&C Heidsieck wine as good as
most grandes marques.

ITALY

8 Italia Collezione Prosecco Brut £11.99
Soft fruit and mousse but refreshingly dry and brisk, it
works well.

What wine
words mean

Wine labels are getting crowded. It's mostly thanks to the unending torrent of new regulation. Lately, for example, the European Union has decided that all wines sold within its borders must display a health warning: 'Contains Sulphites'. All wines are made with the aid of preparations containing sulphur to combat diseases in the vineyards and bacterial infections in the winery. You can't make wine without sulphur. Even 'organic' wines are made with it. But some people are sensitive to the traces of sulphur in some wines, so we must all be informed of the presence of this hazardous material.

That's the way it is. And it might not be long before some even sterner warnings will be added about another ingredient in wine. Alcohol is the new tobacco, as the regulators see it, and in the near future we can look forward to some stern admonishments about the effects of alcohol. In the meantime, the mandatory information on every label includes the quantity, alcoholic strength and country of origin, along with the name of the producer. The region will be specified, vaguely on wines from loosely regulated countries such as Australia, and precisely on wines from over-regulated countries such as France. Wines from 'classic' regions of Europe – Bordeaux, Chianti, Rioja and so on – are mostly labelled according to their location rather than their constituent grape varieties. If it says Sancerre, it's taken as read that you either know it's made with Sauvignon Blanc grapes, or don't care.

Wines from just about everywhere else make no such assumptions. If a New Zealand wine is made from Sauvignon Blanc grapes, you can be sure the label will say so. This does quite neatly represent the gulf between the two worlds of winemaking. In traditional European regions, it's the place, the vineyard, that mostly determines the character of the wines. The French call it *terroir*, to encapsulate not just the lie of the land and the soil conditions but the wild variations in the weather from year to year as well. The grapes are merely the medium through which the timeless mysteries of the deep earth are translated into the ineffable glories of the wine, adjusted annually according to the vagaries of climate, variable moods of the winemaker, and who knows what else.

In the less arcane vineyards of the New World, the grape is definitely king. In hot valleys such as the Barossa (South Australia) or the Maipo (Chile), climate is relatively predictable and the soil conditions are managed by irrigation. It's the fruit that counts, and the style of the wine is determined by the variety – soft, spicy Shiraz; peachy, yellow Chardonnay and so on.

The main purpose of this glossary is, consequently, to give short descriptions of the 'classic' wines, including the names of the grapes they are made from, and of the 70-odd distinct grape varieties that make most of the world's wines. As well as these very brief descriptions, I have included equally shortened summaries of the regions and appellations of the better-known wines, along with some of the local terms used to indicate style and alleged qualities.

Finally, I have tried to explain in simple and rational terms the peculiar words I use in trying to convey the characteristics of wines described. 'Delicious' might need no further qualification, but the likes of 'bouncy', 'green' and 'liquorous' probably do.

A

abboccato – Medium-dry white wine style. Italy, especially Orvieto.

AC – *See* Appellation d'Origine Contrôlée.

acidity – To be any good, every wine must have the right level of acidity. It gives wine the element of dryness or sharpness it needs to prevent cloying sweetness or dull wateriness. If there is too much acidity, wine tastes raw or acetic (vinegary). Winemakers strive to create balanced acidity – either by cleverly controlling the natural processes, or by adding sugar and acid to correct imbalances.

aftertaste – The flavour that lingers in the mouth after swallowing the wine.

Aglianico – Black grape variety of southern Italy. It has romantic associations. When the ancient Greeks first colonised Italy in the seventh century BC, it was with the prime purpose of planting it as a vineyard (the Greek name for Italy was *Oenotria* – land of cultivated vines). The name for the vines the Greeks brought with them was Ellenico (as in Hellas, Greece), from which Aglianico is the modern rendering. To return to the point, these ancient vines, especially in the arid volcanic landscapes of Basilicata and Cilento, produce excellent dark, earthy and highly distinctive wines. A name to look out for.

Agriculture biologique – On French wine labels, an indication that the wine has been made by organic methods.

Albariño – White grape variety of Spain that makes intriguingly perfumed fresh and spicy dry wines, especially in esteemed Rias Baixas region.

alcohol – The alcohol levels in wines are expressed in terms of alcohol by volume ('abv'), that is, the percentage of the volume of the wine that is common, or ethyl, alcohol. A typical wine at 12 per cent abv is thus 12 parts alcohol and, in effect, 88 parts fruit juice.

The question of how much alcohol we can drink without harming ourselves in the short or long term is an impossible one to answer, but there is more or less general agreement among scientists that small amounts of alcohol are good for us, even if the only evidence of this is actuarial – the fact that mortality statistics show teetotallers live significantly shorter lives than moderate drinkers. According to the Department of Health, there are 'safe limits' to the amount of alcohol we should drink weekly. These limits are measured in units of alcohol, with a small glass of wine taken to be one unit. Men are advised that 28 units a week is the most they can drink without risk to health, and for women (whose liver function differs from that of men because of metabolic distinctions) the figure is 21 units.

If you wish to measure your consumption closely, note that a standard 75 cl bottle of wine at 12 per cent alcohol contains 9 units. A bottle of German Moselle at 8 per cent alcohol has only 6 units, but a bottle of Australian Chardonnay at 14 per cent has 10.5.

Alentejo – Wine region of southern Portugal (immediately north of the Algarve), with a fast-improving reputation, especially for sappy, keen reds from local grape varieties including Aragones, Castelão and Trincadeira.

Almansa – DO winemaking region of Spain inland from Alicante, making great-value red wines.

Alsace – France's easternmost wine-producing region lies between the Vosges Mountains and the River Rhine, with Germany beyond. These conditions make for the production of some of the world's most delicious and fascinating white wines, always sold under the name of their constituent grapes. Pinot Blanc is the most affordable – and is well worth looking out for. The 'noble' grape varieties of the region are Gewürztraminer, Muscat, Riesling and Pinot Gris and they are always made on a single-variety basis. The richest, most exotic wines are those from individual *grand* *cru* vineyards, which are named on the label. Some *vendange tardive* (late harvest) wines are made, but tend to be expensive. All the wines are sold in tall, slim green bottles known as flûtes that closely resemble those of the Mosel, and the names of producers and grape varieties are often German too, so it is widely assumed that Alsace wines are German in style, if not in nationality. But this is not the case in either particular. Alsace wines are dry and quite unique in character – and definitely French.

Amarone – Style of red wine made in Valpolicella, Italy. Specially selected grapes are held back from the harvest and stored for several months to dry them out. They are then pressed and fermented into a highly concentrated speciality dry wine. Amarone means 'bitter', describing the dry style of the flavour.

amontillado – *See* sherry.

aperitif – If a wine is thus described, I believe it will give more pleasure before a meal than with one. Crisp, low-alcohol German wines and other delicately flavoured whites (including many dry Italians) are examples.

Appellation d'Origine Contrôlée – Commonly abbreviated to AC or AOC, this is the system under which quality wines are defined in France. About a third of the country's vast annual output qualifies, and there are more than 400 distinct AC zones. The declaration of an AC on the label signifies that the wine meets standards concerning location of vineyards and wineries, grape varieties and limits on harvest per hectare, methods of cultivation and vinification, and alcohol content. Wines are inspected and tasted by state-appointed committees. The one major aspect of any given wine that an AC cannot guarantee is that you will like it – but it certainly improves the chances.

Appellation d'Origine Protégée (AOP) – Under new EU rules of 2010, already incorporated into French law, the AOC system is slowly transforming into AOP. In effect, it will mean little more than the exchange of 'controlled' with 'protected' on labels. One quirk of the new rules is that makers of AOP wines will be able to name the constituent grape variety or varieties on their labels, if they so wish.

Apulia – Anglicised name for Puglia.

Ardèche – Region of southern France to the west of the Rhône valley, home to a good vin de pays zone known as the Coteaux de L'Ardèche. Lots of decent-value reds from Syrah grapes, and some, less interesting, dry whites.

Assyrtiko – White grape variety of Greece now commonly named on dry white wines, sometimes of great quality, from the mainland and islands.

Asti – Town and major winemaking centre in Piedmont, Italy. The sparkling (spumante) sweet wines made from Moscato grapes are inexpensive and often delicious. Typical alcohol level is a modest 5 to 7 per cent.

attack – In wine tasting, the first impression made by the wine in the mouth.

Auslese – German wine-quality designation. *See* QmP.

B

Baga – Black grape variety indigenous to Portugal. Makes famously concentrated, juicy reds that get their deep colour from the grape's particularly thick skins. Look out for this name, now quite frequently quoted as the varietal on Portuguese wine labels. Often very good value for money.

balance – A big word in the vocabulary of wine tasting. Respectable wine must get two key things right: lots of fruitiness from the sweet grape juice, and plenty of acidity so the sweetness is 'balanced' with the crispness familiar in good dry whites and the dryness that marks out good reds. Some wines are noticeably 'well balanced' in that they have memorable fruitiness and the clean, satisfying 'finish' (last flavour in the mouth) that ideal acidity imparts.

Barbera – Black grape variety originally of Piedmont in Italy. Most commonly seen as Barbera d'Asti, the vigorously fruity red wine made around Asti – once better known for sweet sparkling Asti Spumante. Barbera grapes are now being grown in South America, often producing a sleeker, smoother style than at home in Italy.

Bardolino – Once fashionable, light red wine DOC of Veneto, north-west Italy. Bardolino is made principally from Corvina Veronese grapes plus Rondinella, Molinara and Negrara. Best wines are supposed to be those labelled Bardolino Superiore, a DOCG created in 2002. This classification closely specifies the permissible grape varieties and sets the alcohol level at a minimum of 12 per cent.

Barossa Valley – Famed vineyard region north of Adelaide, Australia, produces hearty reds principally from Shiraz, Cabernet Sauvignon and Grenache grapes, plus plenty of lush white wine from Chardonnay. Also known for limey, long-lived, mineral dry whites from Riesling grapes.

barrique – Barrel in French. *En barrique* on a wine label signifies the wine has been matured in oak.

Beaujolais – Unique red wines from the southern reaches of Burgundy, France, are made from Gamay grapes. Beaujolais nouveau, now deeply unfashionable, provides a friendly introduction to the bouncy, red-fruit style of the wine, but for the authentic experience, go for Beaujolais Villages, from the region's better, northern vineyards. There are ten AC zones within this northern sector making wines under their own names. Known as the *crus*, these are Brouilly, Chénas, Chiroubles, Côte de Brouilly, Fleurie, Juliénas, Morgon, Moulin à Vent, Regnié and St Amour and produce most of the best wines of the region. Prices are higher than those for Beaujolais Villages, but by no means always justifiably so.

Beaumes de Venise – Village near Châteauneuf du Pape in France's Rhône valley, famous for sweet and alcoholic wine from Muscat grapes. Delicious, grapey wines. A small number of growers also make strong (sometimes rather tough) red wines under the village name.

Beaune – One of the two winemaking centres (the other is Nuits St Georges) at the heart of Burgundy in France. Three of the region's humbler appellations take the name of the town: Côtes de Beaune, Côtes de Beaune Villages and Hautes Côtes de Beaune. Wines made under these ACs are often, but by no means always, good value for money.

berry fruit – Some red wines deliver a burst of flavour in the mouth that corresponds to biting into a newly picked berry – strawberry, blackberry, etc. So a wine described as having berry fruit (by this writer, anyway) has freshness, liveliness and immediate appeal.

bianco – White wine, Italy.

Bical – White grape variety principally of Dão region of northern Portugal. Not usually identified on labels, because most of it goes into inexpensive sparkling wines. Can make still wines of very refreshing crispness.

biodynamics – A cultivation method taking the organic approach several steps further. Biodynamic winemakers plant and tend their vineyards according to a date and time calendar 'in harmony' with the movements of the planets. Some of France's best-known wine estates subscribe, and many more are going that way. It might all sound bonkers, but it's salutary to learn that biodynamics is based on principles first described by a very eminent man, the Austrian educationist Rudolph Steiner. He's lately been in the news for having written, in 1919, that farmers crazy enough to feed animal products to cattle would drive the livestock 'mad'.

bite – In wine tasting, the impression on the palate of a wine with plenty of acidity and, often, tannin.

blanc – White wine, France.

blanc de blancs – White wine from white grapes, France. May seem to be stating the obvious, but some white wines (e.g. champagne) are made, partially or entirely, from black grapes.

blanc de noirs – White wine from black grapes, France. Usually sparkling (especially champagne) made from black Pinot Meunier and Pinot Noir grapes, with no Chardonnay or other white varieties.

blanco – White wine, Spain and Portugal.

Blauer Zweigelt – Black grape variety of Austria, making a large proportion of the country's red wines, some of excellent quality.

Bobal – Black grape variety mostly of south-eastern Spain. Thick skin is good for colour and juice contributes acidity to blends.

bodega – In Spain, a wine producer or wine shop.

Bonarda – Black grape variety of northern Italy. Now more widely planted in Argentina, where it makes rather elegant red wines, often representing great value.

botrytis – Full name, *botrytis cinerea*, is that of a beneficent fungus that can attack ripe grape bunches late in the season, shrivelling the berries to a gruesome-looking mess, which yields concentrated juice of prized sweetness. Cheerfully known as 'noble rot', this fungus is actively encouraged by winemakers in regions as diverse as Sauternes (in Bordeaux), Monbazillac (in Bergerac), the Rhine and Mosel valleys, Hungary's Tokaji region and South Australia to make ambrosial dessert wines.

bouncy – The feel in the mouth of a red wine with young, juicy fruitiness. Good Beaujolais is bouncy, as are many north-west-Italian wines from Barbera and Dolcetto grapes.

Bourgogne Grand Ordinaire – Appellation of France's Burgundy region for 'ordinary' red and rosé wines from either Gamay or Pinot Noir grapes, or both, and whites from Chardonnay or Aligoté. Some good-value wines, especially from the Buxy co-operative in the southern Chalonnais area.

Bourgueil – Appellation of Loire Valley, France. Long-lived red wines from Cabernet Franc grapes.

briary – In wine tasting, associated with the flavours of fruit from prickly bushes such as blackberries.

brûlé – Pleasant burnt-toffee taste or smell, as in crème brûlée.

brut – Driest style of sparkling wine. Originally French, for very dry champagnes specially developed for the British market, but now used for sparkling wines from all round the world.

Buzet – Little-seen AC of south-west France overshadowed by Bordeaux but producing some characterful ripe reds.

C

Cabardès – Recent AC (1998) for red and rosé wines from area north of Carcassonne, Aude, France. Principally Cabernet Sauvignon and Merlot grapes.

Cabernet Franc – Black grape variety originally of France. It makes the light-bodied and keenly edged red wines of the Loire Valley – such as Chinon and Saumur. And it is much grown in Bordeaux, especially in the appellation of St Emilion. Also now planted in Argentina, Australia and North America. Wines, especially in the Loire, are characterised by a leafy, sappy style and bold fruitiness. Most are best enjoyed young.

Cabernet Sauvignon – Black (or, rather, blue) grape variety now grown in virtually every wine-producing nation. When perfectly ripened, the grapes are smaller than many other varieties and have particularly thick skins. This means that when pressed, Cabernet grapes have a high proportion of skin to juice – and that makes for wine with lots of colour and tannin. In Bordeaux, the grape's traditional home, the grandest Cabernet-based wines have always been known as *vins de garde* (wines to keep) because they take years, even decades, to evolve as the effect of all that skin extraction preserves the fruit all the way to magnificent maturity. But in today's impatient world, these grapes are exploited in modern winemaking techniques to produce the sublime flavours of mature Cabernet without having to hang around for lengthy periods awaiting maturation. While there's nothing like a fine, ten-year-old claret (and nothing quite as expensive), there are many excellent Cabernets from around the world that amply illustrate this grape's characteristics. Classic smells and flavours include blackcurrants, cedar wood, chocolate, tobacco – even violets.

Cahors – An AC of the Lot Valley in south-west France once famous for 'black wine'. This was a curious concoction of straightforward wine mixed with a soupy must, made by boiling up new-pressed juice to concentrate it (through evaporation) before fermentation. The myth is still perpetuated that Cahors wine continues to be made in this way, but production on this basis actually ceased 150 years ago. Cahors today is no stronger, or blacker, than the wines of neighbouring appellations.

Cairanne – Village of the appellation collectively known as the Côtes du Rhône in southern France. Cairanne is one of several villages entitled to put their name on the labels of wines made within their AC boundary, and the appearance of this name is quite reliably an indicator of a very good wine indeed.

Calatayud – DO (quality wine zone) near Zaragoza in the Aragon region of northern Spain where they're making some astonishingly good wines at bargain prices, mainly reds from Garnacha and Tempranillo grapes. These are the varieties that go into the light and oaky wines of Rioja, but in Calatayud, the wines are dark, dense and decidedly different.

Cannonau – Black grape native to Sardinia by name, but in fact the same variety as the ubiquitous Grenache of France (and Garnacha of Spain).

cantina sociale – *See* Co-op.

Carignan – Black grape variety of Mediterranean France. It is rarely identified on labels, but is a major constituent of wines from the southern Rhône and Languedoc-Roussillon regions. Known as Carignano in Italy and Cariñena in Spain.

Cariñena – A region of north-east Spain, south of Navarra, known for substantial reds, as well as the Spanish name for the Carignan grape (*qv*).

Carmenère – Black grape variety once widely grown in Bordeaux but abandoned due to cultivation problems. Lately revived in South America where it is producing fine wines, sometimes with echoes of Bordeaux.

cassis – As a tasting note, signifies a wine that has a noticeable blackcurrant-concentrate flavour or smell. Much associated with the Cabernet Sauvignon grape.

Castelao – Portuguese black grape variety. Same as Periquita.

Catarratto – White grape variety of Sicily. In skilled hands it can make anything from keen, green-fruit dry whites to lush, oaked super-ripe styles. Also used for Marsala.

cat's pee – In tasting notes, a mildly jocular reference to a certain style of Sauvignon Blanc wine.

cava – The sparkling wine of Spain. Most originates in Catalonia, but the Denominación de Origen (DO) guarantee of authenticity is open to producers in many regions of the country. Much cava is very reasonably priced even though it is made by the same method as champagne – second fermentation in bottle, known in Spain as the *método clásico*.

CdR – Côtes du Rhône.

Cépage – Grape variety, French. 'Cépage Merlot' on a label simply means the wine is made largely or exclusively from Merlot grapes.

Chablis – Northernmost AC of France's Burgundy region. Its dry white wines from Chardonnay grapes are known for their fresh and steely style, but the best wines also age very gracefully into complex classics.

Chambourcin – Sounds like a cream cheese but it's a relatively modern (1963) French hybrid black grape that makes some good non-appellation lightweight-but-concentrated reds in the Loire Valley and now some heftier versions in Australia.

Chardonnay – The world's most popular grape variety. Said to originate from the village of Chardonnay in the Mâconnais region of southern Burgundy, the vine is now planted in every wine-producing nation. Wines are commonly characterised by generous colour and sweet-apple smell, but styles range from lean and sharp to opulently rich. Australia started the craze for oaked Chardonnay, the gold-coloured, super-ripe, buttery 'upfront' wines that are a caricature of lavish and outrageously expensive burgundies such as Meursault and Puligny-Montrachet. Rich to the point of egginess, these Aussie pretenders are now giving way to a sleeker, more minerally style with much less oak presence – if any at all. California and Chile, New Zealand and South Africa are competing hard to imitate the Burgundian style, and Australia's success in doing so.

Châteauneuf du Pape – Famed appellation centred on a picturesque village of the southern Rhône valley in France where in the 1320s French Pope Clement V had a splendid new château built for himself as a country retreat amidst his vineyards. The red wines of the AC, which can be made from 13 different grape varieties but principally Grenache, Syrah and Mourvèdre, are regarded as the best of the southern Rhône and have become rather expensive

– but they can be sensationally good. Expensive white wines are also made.

Chenin Blanc – White grape variety of the Loire Valley, France. Now also grown farther afield, especially in South Africa. Makes dry, soft white wines and also rich, sweet styles. Sadly, many low-cost Chenin wines are bland and uninteresting.

cherry – In wine tasting, either a pale red colour or, more commonly, a smell or flavour akin to the sun-warmed, bursting sweet ripeness of cherries. Many Italian wines, from lightweights such as Bardolino and Valpolicella to serious Chianti, have this character. 'Black cherry' as a description is often used of Merlot wines – meaning they are sweet but have a firmness associated with the thicker skins of black cherries.

Cinsault – Black grape variety of southern France, where it is invariably blended with others in wines of all qualities ranging from vin de pays to the pricy reds of Châteauneuf du Pape. Also much planted in South Africa. The effect in wine is to add keen aromas (sometimes compared with turpentine!) and softness to the blend. The name is often spelt Cinsaut.

Clape, La – A small *cru* (defined quality-vineyard area) within the Coteaux du Languedoc where the growers make some seriously delicious red wines, mainly from Carignan, Grenache and Syrah grapes. A name worth looking out for on labels from the region.

claret – The red wine of Bordeaux, France. It comes from Latin *clarus*, meaning 'clear', recalling a time when the red wines of the region were much lighter in colour than they are now.

clarete – On Spanish labels indicates a pale-coloured red wine. Tinto signifies a deeper hue.

classed growth – English translation of French *cru classé* describes a group of 60 individual wine estates in the Médoc district of Bordeaux, which in 1855 were granted this new status on the basis that their wines were the most expensive at that time. The classification was a promotional wheeze to attract attention to the Bordeaux stand at that year's Great Exhibition in Paris. Amazingly, all of the 60 wines concerned are still in production and most still occupy more or less their original places in the pecking order price-wise. The league was divided up into five divisions from *Premier Grand Cru Classé* (just four wines originally, with one promoted in 1971 – the only change ever made to the classification) to *Cinquième Grand Cru Classé*. Other regions of Bordeaux, notably Graves and St Emilion, have since imitated Médoc and introduced their own rankings of *cru classé* estates.

classic – An overused term in every respect – wine descriptions being no exception. In this book, the word is used to describe a very good wine of its type. So, a 'classic' Cabernet Sauvignon is one that is recognisably and admirably characteristic of that grape.

Classico – Under Italy's wine laws, this word appended to the name of a DOC zone has an important significance. The classico wines of the region can only be made from vineyards lying in the best-rated areas, and wines thus labelled (e.g. Chianti Classico, Soave Classico, Valpolicella Classico) can be reliably counted on to be a cut above the rest.

Colombard – White grape variety of southern France. Once employed almost entirely for making the wine that is distilled for armagnac and cognac brandies, but lately restored to varietal prominence in the Vin de Pays des Côtes de Gascogne where high-tech wineries turn it into a fresh and crisp, if unchallenging, dry wine at a budget price. But beware, cheap Colombard (especially from South Africa) can still be very dull.

Conca de Barbera – Winemaking region of Catalonia, Spain.

co-op – Very many of France's good-quality, inexpensive wines are made by co-operatives. These are wine-producing factories whose members, and joint-owners, are local *vignerons* (vine growers). Each year they sell their harvests to the co-op for turning into branded wines. In Italy, co-op wines can be identified by the words *Cantina Sociale* on the label and in Germany by the term *Winzergenossenschaft*.

Corbières – A name to look out for. It's an AC of France's Midi (deep south) and produces countless robust reds and a few interesting whites, often at bargain prices.

Cortese – White grape variety of Piedmont, Italy. At its best, makes amazingly delicious, keenly brisk and fascinating wines, including those of the Gavi DOCG. Worth seeking out.

Costières de Nîmes – Until 1989, this AC of southern France was known as the Costières de Gard. It forms a buffer between the southern Rhône and Languedoc-Roussillon regions, and makes wines from broadly the same range of grape varieties. It's a name to look out for, the best red wines being notable for their concentration of colour and fruit, with the earthy-spiciness of the better Rhône wines and a likeable liquorice note. A few good white wines, too, and even a decent rosé or two.

Côte – In French, it simply means a side, or slope, of a hill. The implication in wine terms is that the grapes come from a vineyard ideally situated for maximum sunlight, good drainage and the unique soil conditions prevailing on the hill in question. It's fair enough to claim that vines grown on slopes might get more sunlight than those grown on the flat, but there is no guarantee whatsoever that any wine labelled 'Côtes du' this or that is made from grapes grown on a hillside anyway. Côtes du Rhône wines are a case in point. Many 'Côtes' wines come from entirely level vineyards and it is worth remembering that many of the vineyards of Bordeaux, producing most of the world's priciest wines, are little short of prairie-flat. The quality factor is determined much more significantly by the weather and the talents of the winemaker.

Côtes de Blaye – Appellation Contrôlée zone of Bordeaux on the right bank of the River Gironde, opposite the more prestigious Médoc zone of the left bank. Best-rated vineyards qualify for the AC Premières Côtes de Blaye. A couple of centuries ago, Blaye (pronounced 'bligh') was the grander of the two, and even today makes some wines that compete well for quality, and at a fraction of the price of wines from its more fashionable rival across the water.

Côtes de Bourg – AC neighbouring Côtes de Blaye, making red wines of fast-improving quality and value.

Côtes du Luberon – Appellation Contrôlée zone of Provence in south-east France. Wines, mostly red, are similar in style to Côtes du Rhône.

Côtes du Rhône – One of the biggest and best-known appellations of south-east France, covering an area roughly defined by the southern reaches of the valley of the River Rhône. Long notorious for cheap and execrable reds, the Côtes du Rhône AC has lately achieved remarkable improvements in quality at all points along the price scale. Lots of brilliant-value warm and spicy reds, principally from Grenache and Syrah grapes. There are also some white and rosé wines.

Côtes du Rhône Villages – Appellation within the larger Côtes du Rhône AC for wine of supposed superiority made in a number of zones associated with a long list of nominated individual villages.

Côtes du Roussillon – Huge appellation of south-west France known for strong, dark, peppery reds often offering very decent value.

Côtes du Roussillon Villages – Appellation for superior wines from a number of nominated locations within the larger Roussillon AC. Some of these village wines can be of exceptional quality and value.

crianza – Means 'nursery' in Spanish. On Rioja and Navarra wines, the designation signifies a wine that has been nursed through a maturing period of at least a year in oak casks and a further six months in bottle before being released for sale.

cru – A word that crops up with confusing regularity on French wine labels. It means 'the growing' or 'the making' of a wine and asserts that the wine concerned is from a specific vineyard. Under the Appellation Contrôlée rules, countless *crus* are classified in various hierarchical ranks. Hundreds of individual vineyards are described as *premier cru* or *grand cru* in the classic wine regions of Alsace, Bordeaux, Burgundy and Champagne. The common denominator is that the wine can be counted on to be enormously expensive. On humbler wines, the use of the word *cru* tends to be mere decoration.

cru classé – *See* classed growth.

cuve – A vat for wine. French.

cuvée – French for the wine in a *cuve*, or vat. The word is much used on labels to imply that the wine is from just one vat, and thus of unique, unblended character. *Première cuvée* is supposedly the best wine from a given pressing because the grapes have had only the initial, gentle squashing to extract the free-run juice. Subsequent *cuvées* will have been from harsher pressings, grinding the grape pulp to extract the last drop of juice.

D

Dão – Major wine-producing region of northern Portugal now turning out much more interesting reds than it used to – worth looking out for anything made by mega-producer Sogrape.

demi sec – 'Half-dry' style of French (and some other) wines. Beware. It can mean anything from off-dry to cloyingly sweet.

DO – Denominación de Origen, Spain's wine-regulating scheme, similar to France's AC, but older – the first DO region was Rioja, from 1926. DO wines are Spain's best, accounting for a third of the nation's annual production.

DOC – Stands for Denominazione di Origine Controllata, Italy's equivalent of France's AC. The wines are made according to the stipulations of each of the system's 300-plus denominated zones of origin, along with a further 70-odd zones, which enjoy the superior classification of DOCG (DOC with *e Garantita* – guaranteed – appended).

Durif – Rare black grape variety mostly of California, where it is also known as Petite Sirah, but with some plantings in Australia.

E

earthy – A tricky word in the wine vocabulary. In this book, its use is meant to be complimentary. It indicates that the wine somehow suggests the soil the grapes were grown in, even (perhaps a shade too poetically) the landscape in which the vineyards lie. The amazing-value red wines of the torrid, volcanic southernmost regions of Italy are often described as earthy. This is an association with the pleasantly 'scorched' back-flavour in wines made from the ultra-ripe harvests of this near-sub-tropical part of the world.

edge – A wine with edge is one with evident (although not excessive) acidity.

élevé – 'Brought up' in French. Much used on wine labels where the wine has been matured (brought up) in oak barrels, *élevé en fûts de chêne*, to give it extra dimensions.

Entre Deux Mers – Meaning 'between two seas', it's a region lying between the Dordogne and Garonne rivers of Bordeaux, now mainly known for dry white wines from Sauvignon and Semillon grapes.

Estremadura – Wine-producing region occupying Portugal's coastal area north of Lisbon. Lots of interesting wines from indigenous grape varieties, usually at bargain prices. If a label mentions Estremadura, it is a safe rule that there might be something good within.

Extremadura – Minor wine-producing region of western Spain abutting the frontier with Portugal's Alentejo region. Not to be confused with Estremadura of Portugal (above).

F

Falanghina – Revived ancient grape variety of southern Italy now making some superbly fresh and tangy white wines.

Faugères – AC of the Languedoc in south-west France. Source of many hearty, economic reds.

Feteasca – White grape variety widely grown in Romania. Name means 'maiden's grape' and the wine tends to be soft and slightly sweet.

Fiano – White grape variety of the Campania of southern Italy and Sicily, lately revived. It is said to have been cultivated by the ancient Romans for a wine called Apianum.

finish – The last flavour lingering in the mouth after wine has been swallowed.

fino – Pale and very dry style of sherry. You drink it thoroughly chilled – and you don't keep it any longer after opening than other dry white wines. Needs to be fresh to be at its best.

Fitou – One of the first 'designer' wines, it's an appellation in France's Languedoc region, where production is dominated by one huge co-operative, the Vignerons de Mont Tauch. Back in the 1970s, this co-op paid a corporate-image company to come up with a Fitou logo and label-design style, and the wines have prospered ever since. And it's not just packaging – Fitou at all price levels can be very good value, especially from the Mont Tauch co-op.

flabby – Fun word describing a wine that tastes dilute or watery, with insufficient acidity.

fruit – In tasting terms, the fruit is the greater part of the overall flavour of a wine. The wine is (or should be) after all, composed entirely of fruit.

G

Gamay – The black grape that makes all red Beaujolais and some ordinary burgundy. It is a pretty safe rule to avoid Gamay wines from any other region, but there are exceptions.

Garganega – White grape variety of the Veneto region of northeast Italy. Best known as the principal ingredient of Soave, but occasionally included in varietal blends and mentioned as such on labels. Correctly pronounced 'gar-GAN-iga'.

Garnacha – Spanish black grape variety synonymous with Grenache of France. It is blended with Tempranillo to make the red wines of Rioja and Navarra, and is now quite widely cultivated elsewhere in Spain to make grippingly fruity varietals.

garrigue – Arid land of France's deep south giving its name to a style of red wine that notionally evokes the herby, heated, peppery flavours associated with such a landscape. A tricky metaphor!

Gavi – DOCG for dry but rich white wine from Cortese grapes in Piedmont, north-west Italy. Trendy Gavi di Gavi wines tend to be enjoyably lush, but are rather expensive.

Gewürztraminer – One of the great grape varieties of Alsace, France. At their best, the wines are perfumed with lychees and are richly, spicily fruity, yet quite dry. Gewürztraminer from Alsace is almost always relatively expensive, but the grape is also grown with some success in Eastern Europe, Germany, Italy, New Zealand and South America, and sold at more approachable prices. Pronounced 'ge-VOORTS-traminner'.

Givry – AC for red and white wines in the Côte Chalonnaise subregion of Burgundy. Source of some wonderfully natural-tasting reds that might be lighter than those of the more prestigious Côte d'Or to the north, but have great merits of their own. Relatively, the wines are often underpriced.

Glera – Alternative name for Prosecco grape of northern Italy.

Graciano – Black grape variety of Spain that is one of the minor constituents of Rioja. Better known in its own right in Australia where it can make dense, spicy, long-lived red wines.

green – I don't often use this in the pejorative. Green, to me, is a likeable degree of freshness, especially in Sauvignon Blanc wines.

Grenache – The mainstay of the wines of the southern Rhône Valley in France. Grenache is usually the greater part of the mix in Côtes du Rhône reds and is widely planted right across the neighbouring Languedoc-Roussillon region. It's a big-cropping variety that thrives even in the hottest climates and is really a blending grape – most commonly with Syrah, the noble variety of the northern Rhône. Few French wines are labelled with its name, but the grape has caught on in Australia in a big way and it is now becoming a familiar varietal, known for strong, dark liquorous reds. Grenache is the French name for what is originally a Spanish variety, Garnacha.

Grillo – White grape of Sicily said to be among the island's oldest indigenous varieties, pre-dating the arrival of the Greeks in 600 BC. Much used for fortified Marsala, it has lately been revived for interesting, aromatic dry table wines.

grip – In wine-tasting terminology, the sensation in the mouth produced by a wine that has a healthy quantity of tannin in it. A wine with grip is a good wine. A wine with too much tannin, or which is still too young (the tannin hasn't 'softened' with age) is not described as having grip, but as mouth-puckering – or simply undrinkable.

Grolleau – Black grape variety of the Loire Valley principally cultivated for Rosé d'Anjou.

Grüner Veltliner – The 'national' white-wine grape of Austria. In the past it made mostly soft, German-style everyday wines, but now is behind some excellent dry styles, too.

H

halbtrocken – 'Half-dry' in Germany's wine vocabulary. A reassurance that the wine is not some ghastly sugared Liebfraumilch-style confection.

hard – In red wine, a flavour denoting excess tannin, probably due to immaturity.

Haute-Médoc – Extensive AOC of Bordeaux accounting for the greater part of the vineyard area to the north of the city of Bordeaux and west of the Gironde river. The Haut-Médoc incorporates the prestigious commune-AOCs of Listrac, Margaux, Moulis, Pauillac, St Estephe and St Julien.

hock – The wine of Germany's Rhine river valleys. Traditionally, but no longer consistently, it comes in brown bottles, as distinct from the wine of the Mosel river valleys – which comes in green ones.

I

Indicazione Geografica Tipica – Italy's recently instituted wine-quality designation, broadly equivalent to France's vin de pays. The label has to state the geographical location of the vineyard and will often (but not always) state the principal grape varieties from which the wine is made.

Indication Géographique Protégée (IGP) – Introduced to France in 2010 under new EU-wide wine-designation rules, IGP covers the wines hitherto known as vins de pays. Some wines are already being labelled IGP, but established vins de pays producers are unlikely to redesignate their products in a hurry, and are not obliged to do so. Some will abbreviate, so, for example, Vin de Pays d'Oc shortens to Pays d'Oc.

isinglass – A gelatinous material used in fining (clarifying) wine. It is derived from fish bladders and consequently is eschewed by makers of 'vegetarian' wines.

J

jammy – The 'sweetness' in dry red wines is supposed to evoke ripeness rather than sugariness. Sometimes, flavours include a sweetness reminiscent of jam. Usually a fault in the winemaking technique.

Jerez – Wine town of Andalucia, Spain, and home to sherry. The English word 'sherry' is a simple mispronunciation of Jerez.

joven – Young wine, Spanish. In regions such as Rioja, *vino joven* is a synonym for *sin crianza*, which means 'without ageing' in cask or bottle.

Jura – Wine region of eastern France incorporating four AOCs, Arbois, Château-Chalon, Côtes du Jura and L'Etoile. Known for still red, white and rosé wines and sparkling wines as well as exotic *vin de paille* and *vin jaune*.

Juraçon – Appellation for white wines from Courbu and Manseng grapes at Pau, south-west France.

K

Kabinett – Under Germany's bewildering wine-quality rules, this is a classification of a top-quality (QmP) wine. Expect a keen, dry, racy style. The name comes from the cabinet or cupboard in which winemakers traditionally kept their most treasured bottles.

Kekfrankos – Black grape variety of Hungary, particularly the Sopron region, which makes some of the country's more interesting red wines, characterised by colour and spiciness. Same variety as Austria's Blaufrankisch.

L

Ladoix – Unfashionable AC at northern edge of Côtes de Beaune makes some of Burgundy's true bargain reds. A name to look out for.

Lambrusco – The name is that of a black grape variety widely grown across northern Italy. True Lambrusco wine is red, dry and very slightly sparkling, but from the 1980s Britain has been deluged with a strange, sweet manifestation of the style, which has done little to enhance the good name of the original. Good Lambrusco is delicious and fun, but in this country now very hard to find.

Languedoc-Roussillon – Vast area of southern France, including the country's south-west Mediterranean region. The source, now, of many great-value wines from countless ACs and vin de pays zones.

lees – The detritus of the winemaking process that collects in the bottom of the vat or cask. Wines left for extended periods on the lees can acquire extra dimensions of flavour, in particular a 'leesy' creaminess.

legs – The liquid residue left clinging to the sides of the glass after wine has been swirled. The persistence of the legs is an indicator of the weight of alcohol. Also known as 'tears'.

lieu dit – This is starting to appear on French wine labels. It translates as an 'agreed place' and is an area of vineyard defined as of particular character or merit, but not classified under wine law. Usually, the *lieu dit*'s name is stated, with the implication that the wine in question has special value.

liquorice – The pungent slightly burnt flavours of this once-fashionable confection are detectable in some wines made from very ripe grapes, for example, the Malbec harvested in Argentina and several varieties grown in the very hot vineyards of southernmost Italy. A close synonym is 'tarry'. This characteristic is by no means a fault in red wine, unless very dominant, but it can make for a challenging flavour that might not appeal to all tastes.

liquorous – Wines of great weight and glyceriney texture (evidenced by the 'legs', or 'tears', which cling to the glass after the wine has been swirled) are always noteworthy. The connection with liquor is drawn in respect of the feel of the wine in the mouth, rather than with the higher alcoholic strength of spirits.

Lirac – Village and AOC of southern Rhône Valley, France. A near-neighbour of the esteemed appellation of Châteauneuf du Pape, Lirac makes red wine of comparable depth and complexity, at competitive prices.

Lugana – DOC of Lombardy, Italy, known for a dry white wine that is often of real distinction – rich, almondy stuff from the ubiquitous Trebbiano grape.

M

Macabeo – One of the main grapes used for cava, the sparkling wine of Spain. It is the same grape as Viura.

Mâcon – Town and collective appellation of southern Burgundy, France. Lightweight white wines from Chardonnay grapes and similarly light reds from Pinot Noir and some Gamay. The better ones, and the ones exported, have the AC Mâcon-Villages and there are individual village wines with their own ACs including Mâcon-Clessé, Mâcon-Viré and Mâcon-Lugny.

Malbec – Black grape variety grown on a small scale in Bordeaux, and the mainstay of the wines of Cahors in France's Dordogne region under the name Cot. Now much better known for producing big butch reds in Argentina.

manzanilla – Pale, very dry sherry of Sanlucar de Barrameda, a resort town on the Bay of Cadiz in Spain. Manzanilla is proud to be distinct from the pale, very dry fino sherry of the main producing town of Jerez de la Frontera an hour's drive inland. Drink it chilled and fresh – it goes downhill in an opened bottle after just a few days, even if kept (as it should be) in the fridge.

Margaret River – Vineyard region of Western Australia regarded as ideal for grape varieties including Cabernet Sauvignon. It has a relatively cool climate and a reputation for making sophisticated wines, both red and white.

Marlborough – Best-known vineyard region of New Zealand's South Island has a cool climate and a name for brisk but cerebral Sauvignon Blanc and Chardonnay wines.

Marsanne – White grape variety of the northern Rhône Valley and, increasingly, of the wider south of France. It's known for making well-coloured wines with heady aroma and fruit.

Mataro – Black grape variety of Australia. It's the same as the Mourvèdre of France and Monastrell of Spain.

McLaren Vale – Vineyard region south of Adelaide in south-east Australia. Known for blockbuster Shiraz (and Chardonnay) that can be of great balance and quality from winemakers who keep the ripeness under control.

meaty – Weighty, rich red wine style.

Mendoza – The region to watch in Argentina. Lying to the east of the Andes mountains, just about opposite the best vineyards of Chile on the other side, Mendoza accounts for the bulk of Argentine wine production, with quality improving fast.

Merlot – One of the great black wine grapes of Bordeaux, and now grown all over the world. The name is said to derive from the French *merle*, meaning a blackbird. Characteristics of Merlot-based wines attract descriptions such as 'plummy' and 'plump' with black-cherry aroma. The grapes are larger than most, and thus have less skin in proportion to their flesh. This means the resulting wines have less tannin than wines from smaller-berry varieties such as Cabernet Sauvignon, and are therefore, in the Bordeaux context at least, more suitable for drinking while still relatively young.

middle palate – In wine tasting, the impression given by the wine when it is held in the mouth.

Midi – Catch-all term for the deep south of France west of the Rhône Valley.

mineral – Good dry white wines can have a crispness and freshness that somehow evokes this word. Purity of flavour is a key.

Minervois – AC for (mostly) red wines from vineyards around the town of Minerve in the Languedoc-Roussillon region of France. Often good value. The new Minervois La Livinière AC – a sort of Minervois *grand cru* – is host to some great estates including Château Maris and Vignobles Lorgeril.

Monastrell – Black grape variety of Spain, widely planted in Mediterranean regions for inexpensive wines notable for their high alcohol and toughness – though they can mature into excellent, soft reds. The variety is known in France as Mourvèdre and in Australia as Mataro.

Monbazillac – AC for sweet, dessert wines within the wider appellation of Bergerac in south-west France. Made from the same grape varieties (principally Sauvignon and Semillon) that go into the much costlier counterpart wines of Barsac and Sauternes near Bordeaux, these stickies from botrytis-affected, late-harvested grapes can be delicious and good value for money.

Montalcino – Hill town of Tuscany, Italy, and a DOCG for strong and very long-lived red wines from Brunello grapes. The wines are mostly very expensive. Rosso di Montalcino, a DOC for the humbler wines of the zone, is often a good buy.

Montepulciano – Black grape variety of Italy. Best known in Montepulciano d'Abruzzo, the juicy, purply-black and bramble-fruited red of the Abruzzi region midway down Italy's Adriatic side. Also the grape in the rightly popular hearty reds of Rosso Conero from around Ancona in the Marches. Not to be confused with the hill town of Montepulciano in Tuscany, famous for expensive Vino Nobile di Montepulciano wine.

morello – Lots of red wines have smells and flavours redolent of cherries. Morello cherries, among the darkest coloured and sweetest of all varieties and the preferred choice of cherry-brandy producers, have a distinct sweetness resembled by some wines made from Merlot grapes. A morello whiff or taste is generally very welcome.

Moscatel – Spanish Muscat.

Moscato – *See* Muscat.

Moselle – The wine of Germany's Mosel river valleys, collectively known for winemaking purposes as Mosel-Saar-Ruwer. The wine always comes in slim, green bottles, as distinct from the brown bottles traditionally, but no longer exclusively, employed for Rhine wines.

Mourvèdre – Widely planted black grape variety of southern France. It's an ingredient in many of the wines of Provence, the Rhône and Languedoc, including the ubiquitous Vin de Pays d'Oc. It's a hot-climate vine and the wine is usually blended with other varieties to give sweet aromas and 'backbone' to the mix. Known as Mataro in Australia and Monastrell in Spain.

Muscadet – One of France's most familiar everyday whites, made from a grape called the Melon or Melon de Bourgogne. It comes from vineyards at the estuarial end of the River Loire, and has a sea-breezy freshness about it. The better wines are reckoned to be those from the vineyards in the Sèvre et Maine region, and many are made *sur lie* – 'on the lees' – meaning that the wine is left in contact with the yeasty deposit of its fermentation until just before bottling, in an endeavour to add interest to what can sometimes be an acidic and fruitless style.

Muscat – Grape variety with origins in ancient Greece, and still grown widely among the Aegean islands for the production of sweet white wines. Muscats are the wines that taste more like grape juice than any other – but the high sugar levels ensure they are also among the most alcoholic of wines, too. Known as Moscato in Italy, the grape is much used for making sweet sparkling wines, as in Asti Spumante or Moscato d'Asti. There are several appellations in south-west France for inexpensive Muscats made rather like port, part-fermented before the addition of grape alcohol to halt the conversion of sugar into alcohol, creating a sweet and heady *vin doux naturel*. Dry Muscat wines, when well made, have a delicious sweet aroma but a refreshing, light touch with flavours reminiscent variously of orange blossom, wood smoke and grapefruit.

must – New-pressed grape juice prior to fermentation.

N

Navarra – DO wine-producing region of northern Spain adjacent to, and overshadowed by, Rioja. Navarra's wines can be startlingly akin to their neighbouring rivals, and sometimes rather better value for money.

négociant – In France, a dealer-producer who buys wines from growers and matures and/or blends them for sale under his or her own label. Purists can be a bit sniffy about these entrepreneurs, claiming that only the vine-grower with his or her own winemaking set-up can make truly authentic stuff, but the truth is that many of the best wines of France are *négociant*-produced – especially at the humbler end of the price scale. *Négociants* are often identified on wine labels as *négociant-éleveur* (literally 'dealer-bringer-up') and meaning that the wine has been matured, blended and bottled by the party in question.

Negroamaro – Black grape variety mainly of Apulia, the fast-improving wine region of south-east Italy. Dense, earthy red wines with ageing potential and plenty of alcohol. The grape behind Copertino.

Nerello Mascalese – Black grape of Sicily making light, flavoursome and alcoholic reds.

Nero d'Avola – Black grape variety of Sicily and southern Italy. It makes deep-coloured wines that, given half a chance, can develop intensity and richness with age.

non-vintage – A wine is described as such when it has been blended from the harvests of more than one year. A non-vintage wine is not necessarily an inferior one, but under quality-control regulations around the world, still table wines most usually derive solely from one year's grape crop to qualify for appellation status. Champagnes and sparkling wines are mostly blended from several vintages, as are fortified wines, such as basic port and sherry.

nose – In the vocabulary of the wine-taster, the nose is the scent of a wine. Sounds a bit dotty, but it makes a sensible enough alternative to the rather bald 'smell'. The use of the word 'perfume' implies that the wine smells particularly good. 'Aroma' is used specifically to describe a wine that smells as it should, as in 'this burgundy has the authentic strawberry-raspberry aroma of Pinot Noir'.

O

oak – Most of the world's costliest wines are matured in new or nearly new oak barrels, giving additional opulence of flavour. Of late, many cheaper wines have been getting the oak treatment, too, in older, cheaper casks, or simply by having sacks of oak chippings poured into their steel or fibreglass holding tanks. 'Oak aged' on a label is likely to indicate the latter treatments. But the overtly oaked wines of Australia have in some cases been so overdone that there is now a reactive trend whereby some producers proclaim their wines – particularly Chardonnays – as 'unoaked' on the label, thereby asserting that the flavours are more naturally achieved.

Oltrepo Pavese – Wine-producing zone of Piedmont, north-west Italy. The name means 'south of Pavia across the [river] Po' and the wines, both white and red, can be excellent quality and value for money.

organic wine – As in other sectors of the food industry, demand for organically made wine is – or appears to be – growing. As a rule, a wine qualifies as organic if it comes entirely from grapes grown in vineyards cultivated without the use of synthetic materials, and made in a winery where chemical treatments or additives are shunned with similar vigour. In fact, there are plenty of winemakers in the world using organic methods, but who disdain to label their bottles as such. Wines proclaiming their organic status used to carry the same sort of premium as their counterparts round the corner in the fruit, vegetable and meat aisles. But organic viticulture is now commonplace and there seems little price impact. There is no single worldwide (or even Europe-wide) standard for organic food or wine, so you pretty much have to take the producer's word for it.

P

Pasqua – One of the biggest and, it should be said, best wine producers of the Veneto region of north-west Italy.

Passetoutgrains – Bourgogne Passetoutgrains is a generic appellation of the Burgundy region, France. The word loosely means 'any grapes allowed' and is supposed specifically to designate a red wine made with Gamay grapes as well as Burgundy's principal black variety, Pinot Noir, in a ratio of two parts Gamay to one of Pinot. The wine is usually relatively inexpensive, and relatively uninteresting, too.

Periquita – Black grape variety of southern Portugal. Makes rather exotic spicy reds. Name means 'parrot'.

Petit Verdot – Black grape variety of Bordeaux used to give additional colour, density and spiciness to Cabernet Sauvignon-dominated blends. Mostly a minority player at home, but in Australia and California it is grown as the principal variety for some big hearty reds of real character.

petrol – When white wines from certain grapes, especially Riesling, are allowed to age in the bottle for longer than a year or two, they can take on a spirity aroma reminiscent of petrol or diesel. In grand mature German wines, this is considered a very good thing.

Picpoul – Grape variety of southern France. Best known in Picpoul de Pinet, a dry white from near Carcassonne in the Languedoc. The name Picpoul means 'stings the lips' – referring to the natural high acidity of the juice.

Piemonte – North-western province of Italy, which we call Piedmont, known for the spumante wines of the town of Asti, plus expensive Barbaresco and Barolo and better-value varietal red wines from Barbera and Dolcetto grapes.

Pinotage – South Africa's own black grape variety. Makes red wines ranging from light and juicy to dark, strong and long-lived. It's a cross between Pinot Noir and a grape the South Africans used to call Hermitage (thus the portmanteau name) but turns out to have been Cinsault.

Pinot Blanc – White grape variety principally of Alsace, France. Florally perfumed, exotically fruity dry white wines.

Pinot Grigio – White grape variety of northern Italy. Wines bearing its name are perplexingly fashionable. Good examples have an interesting smoky-pungent aroma and keen, slaking fruit. But most are dull. Originally French, it is at its best in the lushly exotic Pinot Gris wines of Alsace and is also successfully cultivated in Germany and New Zealand.

Pinot Noir – The great black grape of Burgundy, France. It makes all the region's fabulously expensive red wines. Notoriously difficult to grow in warmer climates, it is nevertheless cultivated by countless intrepid winemakers in the New World intent on reproducing the magic appeal of red burgundy. California and New Zealand have come closest, but rarely at prices much below those for the real thing. Some Chilean Pinot Noirs are inexpensive and worth trying.

Pouilly Fuissé – Village and AC of the Mâconnais region of southern Burgundy in France. Dry white wines from Chardonnay grapes. Wines are among the highest rated of the Mâconnais.

Pouilly Fumé – Village and AC of the Loire Valley in France. Dry white wines from Sauvignon Blanc grapes. Similar 'pebbly', 'grassy' or even 'gooseberry' style to neighbouring AC Sancerre. The notion put about by some enthusiasts that Pouilly Fumé is 'smoky' is surely nothing more than word association with the name.

Primitivo – Black grape variety of southern Italy, especially the region of Puglia. Named from Latin *primus* for first, the grape is among the earliest-ripening of all varieties. The wines are typically dense and dark in colour with plenty of alcohol, and have an earthy, spicy style. Often a real bargain.

Prosecco – White grape variety of Italy's Veneto region known entirely for the softly sparkling wine it makes. The best come from the DOC Conegliano-Valdobbiadene, made as spumante ('foaming') wines in pressurised tanks, typically to 11 per cent alcohol and ranging from softly sweet to crisply dry. Now trendy, but the cheap wines – one leading brand comes in a can – are of very variable quality.

Puglia – The region occupying the 'heel' of southern Italy, lately making many good, inexpensive wines from indigenous grape varieties.

Q

QbA – German, standing for Qualitätswein bestimmter Anbaugebiete. It means 'quality wine from designated areas' and implies that the wine is made from grapes with a minimum level of ripeness, but it's by no means a guarantee of exciting quality. Only wines labelled QmP (see next entry) can be depended upon to be special.

QmP – Stands for Qualitätswein mit Prädikat. These are the serious wines of Germany, made without the addition of sugar to 'improve' them. To qualify for QmP status, the grapes must reach a level of ripeness as measured on a sweetness scale – all according to Germany's fiendishly complicated wine-quality regulations. Wines from grapes that reach the stated minimum level of sweetness qualify for the description of Kabinett. The next level up earns the rank of Spätlese, meaning 'late-picked'. Kabinett wines can be expected to be dry and brisk in style, and Spätlese wines a little bit riper and fuller. The next grade up, Auslese, meaning 'selected harvest', indicates a wine made from super-ripe grapes; it will be golden in colour and honeyed in flavour. A generation ago, these wines were as valued, and as expensive, as any of the world's grandest appellations, but the collapse in demand for German wines in the UK – brought about by the disrepute rightly earned for floods of filthy Liebfraumilch – means they are now seriously undervalued.

Quincy – AC of Loire Valley, France, known for pebbly-dry white wines from Sauvignon grapes. The wines are forever compared to those of nearby and much better-known Sancerre – and Quincy often represents better value for money. Pronounced 'KAN-see'.

Quinta – Portuguese for farm or estate. It precedes the names of many of Portugal's best-known wines. It is pronounced 'KEEN-ta'.

R

racy – Evocative wine-tasting description for wine that thrills the tastebuds with a rush of exciting sensations. Good Rieslings often qualify.

raisiny – Wines from grapes that have been very ripe or overripe at harvest can take on a smell and flavour akin to the concentrated, heat-dried sweetness of raisins. As a minor element in the character of a wine, this can add to the appeal but as a dominant characteristic it is a fault.

rancio – Spanish term harking back to Roman times when wines were commonly stored in jars outside, exposed to the sun, so they oxidised and took on a burnt sort of flavour. Today, *rancio* describes a baked – and by no means unpleasant – flavour in fortified wines, particularly sherry and Madeira.

Reserva – In Portugal and Spain, this has genuine significance. The Portuguese use it for special wines with a higher alcohol level and longer ageing, although the precise periods vary between regions. In Spain, especially in the Navarra and Rioja regions, it means the wine must have had at least a year in oak and two in bottle before release.

reserve – On French (as *réserve*) or other wines, this implies special-quality, longer-aged wines, but has no official significance.

Retsina – The universal white wine of Greece. It has been traditionally made in Attica, the region of Athens, for a very long time, and is said to owe its origins and name to the ancient custom of sealing amphorae (terracotta jars) of the wine with a gum made from pine resin. Some of the flavour of the resin inevitably transmitted itself into the wine, and ancient Greeks acquired a lasting taste for it.

Reuilly – AC of Loire Valley, France, for crisp dry whites from Sauvignon grapes. Pronounced 'RER-yee'.

Ribatejo – Emerging wine region of Portugal. Worth seeking out on labels of red wines in particular, because new winemakers are producing lively stuff from distinctive indigenous grapes such as Castelao and Trincadeira.

Ribera del Duero – Classic wine region of north-west Spain lying along the River Duero (which crosses the border to become

Portugal's Douro, forming the valley where port comes from). It is home to an estate rather oddly named Vega Sicilia, where red wines of epic quality are made and sold at equally epic prices. Further down the scale, some very good reds are made, too.

Riesling – The noble grape variety of Germany. It is correctly pronounced 'REEZ-ling', not 'RICE-ling'. Once notorious as the grape behind all those boring 'medium' Liebfraumilches and Niersteiners, this grape has had a bad press. In fact, there has never been much, if any, Riesling in Germany's cheap-and-nasty plonks. But the country's best wines, the so-called Qualitätswein mit Prädikat grades, are made almost exclusively with Riesling. These wines range from crisply fresh and appley styles to extravagantly fruity, honeyed wines from late-harvested grapes. Excellent Riesling wines are also made in Alsace and now in Australia.

Rioja – The principal fine-wine region of Spain, in the country's north east. The pricier wines are noted for their vanilla-pod richness from long ageing in oak casks. Tempranillo and Garnacha grapes make the reds, Viura the whites.

Ripasso – A particular style of Valpolicella wine. New wine is partially refermented in vats that have been used to make the Recioto reds (wines made from semi-dried grapes), thus creating a bigger, smoother version of usually light and pale Valpolicella.

Riserva – In Italy, a wine made only in the best vintages, and allowed longer ageing in cask and bottle.

Rivaner – Alternative name for Germany's Müller-Thurgau grape, the life-blood of Liebfraumilch.

Riverland – Vineyard region to the immediate north of the Barossa Valley of South Australia, extending east into New South Wales.

Roditis – White grape variety of Greece, known for fresh dry whites with decent acidity, often included in retsina.

rosso – Red wine, Italy.

Rosso Conero – DOC red wine made in the environs of Ancona in the Marches, Italy. Made from the Montepulciano grape, the wine can provide excellent value for money.

Ruby Cabernet – Black grape variety of California, created by crossing Cabernet Sauvignon and Carignan. Makes soft and squelchy red wine at home and in South Africa.

Rueda – DO of north-west Spain making first-class refreshing dry whites from the indigenous Verdejo grape, imported Sauvignon, and others. Exciting quality, and prices are keen.

Rully – AC of Chalonnais region of southern Burgundy, France. White wines from Chardonnay and red wines from Pinot Noir grapes. Both can be very good and are substantially cheaper than their more northerly Burgundian neighbours. Pronounced 'ROO-yee'.

S

Saint Emilion – AC of Bordeaux, France. Centred on the romantic hill town of St Emilion, this famous sub-region makes some of the grandest red wines of France, but also some of the best-value ones. Less fashionable than the Médoc region on the opposite (west) bank of the River Gironde that bisects Bordeaux, St Emilion wines are made largely with the Merlot grape, and are relatively quick to mature. The grandest wines are classified *1er grand cru classé* and are madly expensive, but many more are classified respectively *grand cru classé* and *grand cru*, and these designations can be seen as a fairly trustworthy indicator of quality. There are several 'satellite' St Emilion ACs named after the villages at their centres, notably Lussac St Emilion, Montagne St Emilion and Puisseguin St Emilion. Some excellent wines are made by estates within these ACs, and at relatively affordable prices thanks to the comparatively humble status of their satellite designations.

Salento – Up-and-coming wine region of southern Italy. Many good bargain reds from local grapes including Nero d'Avola and Primitivo.

Sancerre – AC of the Loire Valley, France, renowned for flinty-fresh Sauvignon whites and rarer Pinot Noir reds. These wines are never cheap, and recent tastings make it plain that only the best-made, individual-producer wines are worth the money. Budget brands seem mostly dull.

Sangiovese – The local black grape of Tuscany, Italy. It is the principal variety used for Chianti and is now widely planted in Latin America – often making delicious, Chianti-like wines with characteristic cherryish-but-deeply-ripe fruit and a dry, clean finish. Chianti wines have become (unjustifiably) expensive in recent years and cheaper Italian wines such as those called Sangiovese di Toscana make a consoling substitute.

Saumur – Town and appellation of Loire Valley, France. Characterful minerally red wines from Cabernet Franc grapes, and some whites. The once-popular sparkling wines from Chenin Blanc grapes are now little seen in Britain.

Saumur-Champigny – Separate appellation for red wines from Cabernet Franc grapes of Saumur in the Loire, sometimes very good and lively.

Sauvignon Blanc – French white grape variety now grown worldwide. New Zealand is successfully challenging the long supremacy of French ACs such as Sancerre. The wines are characterised by aromas of gooseberry, fresh-cut grass, even asparagus. Flavours are often described as 'grassy' or 'nettly'.

sec – Dry wine style. French.

secco – Dry wine style. Italian.

Semillon – White grape variety originally of Bordeaux, where it is blended with Sauvignon Blanc to make fresh dry whites and, when harvested very late in the season, the ambrosial sweet whites of Barsac, Sauternes and other appellations. Even in the driest wines, the grape can be recognised from its honeyed, sweet-pineapple, even banana-like aromas. Now widely planted in Australia and Latin America, and frequently blended with Chardonnay to make dry whites, some of them interesting.

sherry – The great aperitif wine of Spain, centred on the Andalusian city of Jerez (from which the name 'sherry' is an English mispronunciation). There is a lot of sherry-style wine in the world, but only the authentic wine from Jerez and the neighbouring producing towns of Puerta de Santa Maria and Sanlucar de Barrameda may label their wines as such. The Spanish drink real sherry – very dry and fresh, pale in colour and served well-chilled – called fino and manzanilla, and darker but naturally dry variations called amontillado, palo cortado and oloroso.

Shiraz – Australian name for the Syrah grape. The variety is the most widely planted of any in Australia, and makes red wines of wildly varying quality, characterised by dense colour, high alcohol, spicy fruit and generous, cushiony texture.

Somontano – Wine region of north-east Spain. Name means 'under the mountains' – in this case the Pyrenees – and the region has had DO status since 1984. Much innovative winemaking here, with New World styles emerging. Some very good buys. A region to watch.

souple – French wine-tasting term that translates into English as 'supple' or even 'docile' as in 'pliable', but I understand it in the vinous context to mean muscular but soft – a wine with tannin as well as soft fruit.

Spätlese – *See* QmP.

spirity – Some wines, mostly from the New World, are made from grapes so ripe at harvest that their high alcohol content can be detected through a mildly burning sensation on the tongue, similar to the effect of sipping a spirit.

spritzy – Describes a wine with a barely detectable sparkle. Some young wines are intended to have this elusive fizziness; in others it is a fault.

spumante – Sparkling wine of Italy. Asti Spumante is the best known, from the town of Asti in the north-west Italian province of Piemonte. The term describes wines that are fully sparkling. Frizzante wines have a less vigorous mousse.

stalky – A useful tasting term to describe red wines with flavours that make you think the stalks from the grape bunches must have been fermented along with the must (juice). Young Bordeaux reds very often have this mild astringency. In moderation it's fine, but if it dominates it probably signifies the wine is at best immature and at worst badly made.

Stellenbosch – Town and region at the heart of South Africa's burgeoning wine industry. It's an hour's drive from Cape Town and the source of much of the country's cheaper wine. Quality is variable, and the name Stellenbosch on a label can't (yet, anyway) be taken as a guarantee of quality.

stony – Wine-tasting term for keenly dry white wines. It's meant to indicate a wine of purity and real quality, with just the right match of fruit and acidity.

structured – Good wines are not one-dimensional, they have layers of flavour and texture. A structured wine has phases of enjoyment: the 'attack', or first impression in the mouth; the middle palate as the wine is held in the mouth; and the lingering aftertaste.

summer fruit – Wine-tasting term intended to convey a smell or taste of soft fruits such as strawberries and raspberries – without having to commit too specifically to which.

superiore – On labels of Italian wines, this is more than an idle boast. Under DOC rules, wines must qualify for the *superiore* designation by reaching one or more specified quality levels, usually a higher alcohol content or an additional period of maturation. Frascati, for example, qualifies for DOC status at 11.5 per cent alcohol, but to be classified *superiore* must have 12 per cent alcohol.

sur lie – Literally, 'on the lees'. It's a term now widely used on the labels of Muscadet wines, signifying that after fermentation has died down, the new wine has been left in the tank over the winter on the lees – the detritus of yeasts and other interesting compounds left over from the turbid fermentation process. The idea is that additional interest is imparted into the flavour of the wine.

Syrah – The noble grape of the Rhône Valley, France. Makes very dark, dense wine characterised by peppery, tarry aromas. Now planted all over southern France and farther afield. In Australia, where it makes wines ranging from disagreeably jam-like plonks to wonderfully rich and silky keeping wines, it is known as Shiraz.

T

table wine – Wine that is unfortified and of an alcoholic strength, for UK tax purposes anyway, of no more than 15 per cent. I use the term to distinguish, for example, between the red table wines of the Douro Valley in Portugal and the region's better-known fortified wine, port.

Tafelwein – Table wine, German. The humblest quality designation, which doesn't usually bode very well.

tank method – Bulk-production process for sparkling wines. Base wine undergoes secondary fermentation in a large, sealed vat rather than in individual closed bottles. Also known as the Charmat method after the name of the inventor of the process.

Tannat – Black grape of south-west France, notably for wines of Madiran, and lately named as the variety most beneficial to health thanks to its outstanding antioxidant content.

tannin – Well known as the film-forming, teeth-coating component in tea, tannin is a natural compound that occurs in black grape skins and acts as a natural preservative in wine. Its noticeable presence in wine is regarded as a good thing. It gives young everyday reds their dryness, firmness of flavour and backbone. And it helps high-quality reds to retain their lively fruitiness for many years. A grand Bordeaux red when first made, for example, will have purply-sweet, rich fruit and mouth-puckering tannin, but after ten years or so this will have evolved into a delectably fruity, mature wine in which the formerly parching effects of the tannin have receded almost completely, leaving the shade of 'residual tannin' that marks out a great wine approaching maturity.

Tarrango – Black grape variety of Australia.

tarry – On the whole, winemakers don't like critics to say their wines evoke the redolence of road repairs, but I can't help using this term to describe the agreeable, sweet, 'burnt' flavour that is often found at the centre of the fruit in wines from Argentina, Italy and Portugal in particular.

TCA – Dreaded ailment in wine, usually blamed on faulty corks. It stands for 246 *trichloroanisol* and is characterised by a horrible musty smell and flavour in the affected wine. It is largely because of the current plague of TCA that so many wine producers worldwide are now going over to polymer 'corks' and screwcaps.

tears – The colourless alcohol in the wine left clinging to the inside of the glass after the contents have been swirled. Persistent tears (also known as 'legs') indicate a wine of good concentration.

Tempranillo – The great black grape of Spain. Along with Garnacha (Grenache in France) it makes all red Rioja and Navarra wines and, under many pseudonyms, is an important or exclusive contributor to the wines of many other regions of Spain. It is also widely cultivated in South America.

tinto – On Spanish labels indicates a deeply coloured red wine. Clarete denotes a paler colour. Also Portuguese.

Toro – Quality wine region east of Zamora, Spain.

Torrontes – White grape variety of Argentina. Makes soft, dry wines often with delicious grapey-spicy aroma, similar in style to the classic dry Muscat wines of Alsace, but at more accessible prices.

Touraine – Region encompassing a swathe of the Loire Valley, France. Non-AC wines may be labelled 'Sauvignon de Touraine' etc.

Touriga Nacional – The most valued black grape variety of the Douro Valley in Portugal, where port is made. The name Touriga now appears on an increasing number of table wines made as sidelines by the port producers. They can be very good, with the same spirity aroma and sleek flavours of port itself, minus the fortification.

Traminer – Grape variety, the same as Gewürztraminer.

Trebbiano – The workhorse white grape of Italy. A productive variety that is easy to cultivate, it seems to be included in just about every ordinary white wine of the entire nation – including Frascati, Orvieto and Soave. It is the same grape as France's Ugni Blanc. There are, however, distinct regional variations of the grape. Trebbiano di Lugana makes a distinctive white in the DOC of the name, sometimes very good, while Trebbiano di Toscana makes a major contribution to the distinctly less interesting dry whites of Chianti country.

Trincadeira Preta – Portuguese black grape variety native to the port-producing vineyards of the Douro Valley (where it goes under the name Tinta Amarella). In southern Portugal, it produces dark and sturdy table wines.

trocken – 'Dry' German wine. It's a recent trend among commercial-scale producers in the Rhine and Mosel to label their wines with this description in the hope of reassuring consumers that the contents do not resemble the dreaded sugar-water Liebfraumilch-type plonks of the bad old days. But the description does have a particular meaning under German wine law, namely that there is only a low level of unfermented sugar lingering in the wine (9 grams per litre, if you need to know), and this can leave the wine tasting rather austere.

U

Ugni Blanc – The most widely cultivated white grape variety of France and the mainstay of many a cheap dry white wine. To date it has been better known as the provider of base wine for distilling into armagnac and cognac, but lately the name has been appearing on wine labels. Technology seems to be improving the performance of the grape. The curious name is pronounced 'OON-yee', and is the same variety as Italy's ubiquitous Trebbiano.

Utiel-Requena – Region and *Denominación de Origen* of Mediterranean Spain inland from Valencia. Principally red wines from Bobal, Garnacha and Tempranillo grapes grown at relatively high altitude, between 600 and 900 metres.

V

Vacqueyras – Village of the southern Rhône Valley of France in the region better known for its generic appellation, the Côtes du Rhône. Vacqueyras can date its winemaking history all the way back to 1414, but has only been producing under its own village AC since 1991. The wines, from Grenache and Syrah grapes, can be wonderfully silky and intense, spicy and long-lived.

Valdepeñas – An island of quality production amidst the ocean of mediocrity that is Spain's La Mancha region – where most of the grapes are grown for distilling into the head-banging brandies of Jerez. Valdepeñas reds are made from a grape they call the Cencibel – which turns out to be a very close relation of the Tempranillo grape that is the mainstay of the fine but expensive red wines of Rioja. Again, like Rioja, Valdepeñas wines are matured in oak casks to give them a vanilla-rich smoothness. Among bargain reds, Valdepeñas is a name to look out for.

Valpolicella – Red wine of Verona, Italy. Good examples have ripe, cherry fruit and a pleasingly dry finish. Unfortunately, there are many bad examples of Valpolicella. Shop with circumspection. Valpolicella Classico wines, from the best vineyards clustered around the town, are more reliable. Those additionally labelled Superiore have higher alcohol and some bottle age.

vanilla – Ageing wines in oak barrels (or, less picturesquely, adding oak chips to wine in huge concrete vats) imparts a range of characteristics including a smell of vanilla from the ethyl vanilline naturally given off by oak.

varietal – A varietal wine is one named after the grape variety (one or more) from which it is made. Nearly all everyday wines worldwide are now labelled in this way. It is salutary to contemplate that just 30 years ago, wines described thus were virtually unknown outside Germany and one or two quirky regions of France and Italy.

vegan-friendly – My informal way of noting that a wine is claimed to have been made not only with animal-product-free finings (*see* Vegetarian wine) but without any animal-related products whatsoever, such as manure in the vineyards.

vegetal – A tasting note definitely open to interpretation. It suggests a smell or flavour reminiscent less of fruit (apple, pineapple, strawberry and the like) than of something leafy or even root based. Some wines are evocative (to some tastes) of beetroot, cabbage or even unlikelier vegetable flavours – and these characteristics may add materially to the attraction of the wine.

vegetarian wine – Wines labelled 'suitable for vegetarians' have been made without the assistance of animal products for 'fining' – clarifying – before bottling. Gelatine, egg whites, isinglass from fish bladders and casein from milk are among the items shunned, usually in favour of bentonite, an absorbent clay first found at Benton in the US state of Montana.

Verdejo – White grape of the Rueda region in north-west Spain. It can make superbly perfumed crisp dry whites of truly distinctive character and has helped make Rueda one of the best white-wine sources of Europe. No relation to Verdelho.

Verdelho – Portuguese grape variety once mainly used for a medium-dry style of Madeira, also called Verdelho, but now rare. The vine is now prospering in Australia, where it can make well-balanced dry whites with fleeting richness and lemon-lime acidity.

Verdicchio – White grape variety of Italy best known in the DOC zone of Castelli dei Jesi in the Adriatic wine region of the Marches. Dry white wines once known for little more than their naff amphora-style bottles but now gaining a reputation for interesting, herbaceous flavours of recognisable character.

Vermentino – White grape variety principally of Italy, especially Sardinia. Makes florally scented soft dry whites.

Vieilles vignes – Old vines. Many French producers like to claim on their labels that the wine within is from vines of notable antiquity. While it's true that vines don't produce useful grapes for the first few years after planting, it is uncertain whether vines of much greater age – say 25 years plus – than others actually make better fruit. There are no regulations governing the use of the term, so it's not a reliable indicator anyway.

Vin Délimité de Qualité Supérieure – Usually abbreviated to VDQS, a French wine-quality designation between appellation contrôlée and vin de pays. To qualify, the wine has to be from approved grape varieties grown in a defined zone. This designation is gradually disappearing.

vin de liqueur – Sweet style of white wine mostly from the Pyrenean region of south-westernmost France, made by adding a little spirit to the new wine before it has fermented out, halting the fermentation and retaining sugar.

vin de pays – 'Country wine' of France. The French map is divided up into more than 100 vin de pays regions. Wine in bottles labelled as such must be from grapes grown in the nominated zone or *département*. Some vin de pays areas are huge: the Vin de Pays d'Oc (named after the Languedoc region) covers much of the Midi and Provence. Plenty of wines bearing this humble designation are of astoundingly high quality and certainly compete with New World counterparts for interest and value. *See* Indication Géographique Protégée.

vin de table – The humblest official classification of French wine. Neither the region, grape varieties nor vintage need be stated on the label. The wine might not even be French. Don't expect too much from this kind of 'table wine'.

vin doux naturel – Sweet, mildly fortified wine of southern France. A little spirit is added during the winemaking process, halting the fermentation by killing the yeast before it has consumed all the sugars – hence the pronounced sweetness of the wine.

vin gris – Rosé wine from Provence.

Vinho de mesa – 'Table wine' of Portugal.

Vino da tavola – The humblest official classification of Italian wine. Much ordinary plonk bears this designation, but the bizarre quirks of Italy's wine laws dictate that some of that country's finest wines are also classed as mere vino da tavola (table wine). If an expensive Italian wine is labelled as such, it doesn't mean it will be a disappointment.

Vino de mesa – 'Table wine' of Spain. Usually very ordinary.

vintage – The grape harvest. The year displayed on bottle labels is the year of the harvest. Wines bearing no date have been blended from the harvests of two or more years.

Viognier – A grape variety once exclusive to the northern Rhône Valley in France where it makes a very chi-chi wine, Condrieu, usually costing £20 plus. Now, the Viognier is grown more widely, in North and South America as well as elsewhere in France, and occasionally produces soft, marrowy whites that echo the grand style of Condrieu itself. The Viognier is now commonly blended with Shiraz in red winemaking in Australia and South Africa. It does not dilute the colour and is confidently believed by highly experienced winemakers to enhance the quality. Steve Webber, in charge of winemaking at the revered De Bortoli estates in the Yarra Valley region of Victoria, Australia, puts between two and five per cent Viognier in with some of his Shiraz wines. 'I think it's the perfume,' he told me. 'It gives some femininity to the wine.'

Viura – White grape variety of Rioja, Spain. Also widely grown elsewhere in Spain under the name Macabeo. Wines have a blossomy aroma and are dry, but sometimes soft at the expense of acidity.

Vouvray – AC of the Loire Valley, France, known for still and sparkling dry white wines and sweet, still whites from late-harvested grapes. The wines, all from Chenin Blanc grapes, have a unique capacity for unctuous softness combined with lively freshness – an effect best portrayed in the demi-sec (slightly sweet) wines, which can be delicious and keenly priced. Unfashionable, but worth looking out for.

Vranac – Black grape variety of the Balkans known for dense colour and tangy-bitter edge to the flavour. Best enjoyed in situ.

W

weight – In an ideal world the weight of a wine is determined by the ripeness of the grapes from which it has been made. In some cases the weight is determined merely by the quantity of sugar added during the production process. A good, genuine wine described as having weight is one in which there is plenty of alcohol and 'extract' – colour and flavour from the grapes. Wine enthusiasts judge weight by swirling the wine in the glass and then examining the 'legs' or 'tears' left clinging to the inside of the glass after the contents have subsided. Alcohol gives these runlets a dense, glycerine-like condition, and if they cling for a long time, the wine is deemed to have weight – a very good thing in all honestly made wines.

Winzergenossenschaft – One of the many very lengthy and peculiar words regularly found on labels of German wines. This means a winemaking co-operative. Many excellent German wines are made by these associations of growers.

woodsap – A subjective tasting note. Some wines have a fleeting bitterness, which is not a fault, but an interesting balancing factor amidst very ripe flavours. The effect somehow evokes woodsap.

X

Xarel-lo – One of the main grape varieties for cava, the sparkling wine of Spain.

Xinomavro – Black grape variety of Greece. It retains its acidity even in the very hot conditions that prevail in many Greek vineyards, where harvests tend to over-ripen and make cooked-tasting wines. Modern winemaking techniques are capable of making well-balanced wines from Xinomavro.

Y

Yecla – Town and DO wine region of eastern Spain, close to Alicante, making lots of interesting, strong-flavoured red and white wines, often at bargain prices.

yellow – White wines are not white at all, but various shades of yellow – or, more poetically, gold. Some white wines with opulent richness even have a flavour I cannot resist calling yellow – reminiscent of butter.

Z

Zinfandel – Black grape variety of California. Makes brambly reds, some of which can age very gracefully, and 'blush' whites – actually pink, because a little of the skin colour is allowed to leach into the must. The vine is also planted in Australia and South America. The Primitivo of southern Italy is said to be a related variety, but makes a very different kind of wine.

—*Making the most of it*—

There has always been a lot of nonsense talked about the correct ways to serve wine. Red wine, we are told, should be opened and allowed to 'breathe' before pouring. White wine should be chilled. Wine doesn't go with soup, tomatoes or chocolate. You know the sort of thing.

It would all be simply laughable except that these daft conventions do make so many potential wine lovers nervous about the simple ritual of opening a bottle and sharing it around. Here is a short and opinionated guide to the received wisdom.

Breathing

Simply uncorking a wine for an hour or two before you serve it will make absolutely no difference to the way it tastes. However, if you wish to warm up an icy bottle of red by placing it near (never on) a radiator or fire, do remove the cork first. As the wine warms, even very slightly, it gives off gas, which will spoil the flavour if it cannot escape.

Chambré-ing

One of the more florid terms in the wine vocabulary. The idea is that red wine should be at the same temperature as the room (chambre) you're going to drink it in. In fairness, it makes sense – although the term harks back to the days when the only people who drank wine were those who could afford to keep it in the freezing cold vaulted cellars beneath their houses. The ridiculously high temperatures to which some homes are raised by central heating systems today are really far too warm for wine. But presumably those who live in such circumstances do so out of choice, and will prefer their wine to be similarly overheated.

Chilling

Drink your white wine as cold as you like. It's certainly true that good whites are at their best at a cool rather than at an icy temperature, but cheap and characterless wines can be improved immeasurably if they are cold enough – the anaesthetising effect of the temperature removes all sense of taste. Pay no attention to notions that red wine should not be served cool. There are plenty of lightweight reds that will respond very well to an hour in the fridge.

Corked wine

Wine trade surveys reveal that far too many bottles are in no fit state to be sold. The villain is very often cited as the cork. Cut from the bark of cork-oak trees cultivated for the purpose in Portugal and Spain, these natural stoppers have done sterling service for 200 years, but now face a crisis of confidence among wine producers. A diseased or damaged cork can make the wine taste stale because air has penetrated, or musty-mushroomy due to TCA, an infection of the raw material. These faults in wine, known as 'corked' or 'corky', should be immediately obvious, even in the humblest bottle, so you should return the bottle to the supplier and demand a refund.

Today, more and more wine producers are opting to close their bottles with polymer bungs. Some are designed to resemble the 'real thing' while others come in a rather disorienting range of colours – including black. While these things can be a pain to extract, there seems to be no evidence they do any harm to the wine. Don't 'lay down' bottles closed with polymer. The potential effects of years of contact with the plastic are yet to be scientifically established.

The same goes for screwcaps. These do have the merit of obviating the struggle with the corkscrew, but prolonged contact of the plastic liner with the wine might not be a good idea.

Corkscrews

The best kind of corkscrew is the 'waiter's friend' type. It looks like a pen-knife, unfolding a 'worm' (the helix or screw) and a lever device which, after the worm has been driven into the cork (try to centre it) rests on the lip of the bottle and enables you to withdraw the cork with minimal effort. Some have two-stage lips to facilitate the task. These devices are cheaper and longer-lasting than any of the more elaborate types, and are equally effective at withdrawing polymer bungs – which can be hellishly difficult to unwind from Teflon-coated 'continuous' corkscrews like the Screwpull.

Decanting

There are two views on the merits of decanting wines. The prevailing one seems to be that it is pointless and even pretentious. The other is that it can make real improvements in the way a wine tastes and is definitely worth the trouble.

Scientists, not usually much exercised by the finer nuances of wine, will tell you that exposure to the air causes wine to 'oxidise' – take in oxygen molecules that will quite quickly initiate the process of turning wine into vinegar – and anyone who has tasted a 'morning-after' glass of wine will no doubt vouch for this.

But the fact that wine does oxidise is a genuine clue to the reality of the effects of exposure to air. Shut inside its bottle, a young wine is very much a live substance, jumping with natural, but mysterious, compounds that can cause all sorts of strange taste sensations. But by exposing the wine to air these effects are markedly reduced.

In wines that spend longer in the bottle, the influence of these factors diminishes, in a process called 'reduction'. In red wines, the hardness of tannin – the natural preservative imparted into wine from the grape skins – gradually reduces, just as the raw purple colour darkens to ruby and later to orangey-brown.

I believe there is less reason for decanting old wines than new, unless the old wine has thrown a deposit and needs carefully to be poured off it. And in some light-bodied wines, such as older Rioja, decanting is probably a bad idea because it can accelerate oxidation all too quickly.

As to actual experiments, I have carried out several of my own, with wines opened in advance or wines decanted compared to the same wines just opened and poured, and my own unscientific judgement is that big, young, alcoholic reds can certainly be improved by aeration.

Washing glasses

If your wine glasses are of any value to you, don't put them in the dishwasher. Over time, they'll craze from the heat of the water. And they will not emerge in the glitteringly pristine condition suggested by the pictures on some detergent packets. For genuinely perfect glasses that will stay that way, wash them in hot soapy water, rinse with clean, hot water and dry immediately with a glass cloth kept exclusively for this purpose. Sounds like fanaticism, but if you take your wine seriously, you'll see there is sense in it.

Keeping wine

How long can you keep an opened bottle of wine before it goes downhill? Not long. A re-corked bottle with just a glassful out of it should stay fresh until the day after, but if there is a lot of air inside the bottle, the wine will oxidise, turning progressively stale and sour. Wine 'saving' devices that allow you to withdraw the air from the bottle via a punctured, self-sealing rubber stopper are variably effective, but don't expect these to keep a wine fresh for more than a couple of re-openings. A crafty method of keeping a half-finished bottle is to decant it, via a funnel, into a clean half bottle and recork.

Storing wine

Supermarket labels always seem to advise that 'this wine should be consumed within one year of purchase'. I think this is a wheeze to persuade customers to drink it up quickly and come back for more. Many of the more robust red wines are likely to stay in good condition for much more than one year, and plenty will actually improve with age. On the other hand, it is a sensible axiom that inexpensive dry white wines are better the younger they are. If you do intend to store wines for longer than a few weeks, do pay heed to the conventional wisdom that bottles are best stored in low, stable temperatures, preferably in the dark. Bottles closed with conventional corks should be laid on their side lest the corks dry out for lack of contact with the wine. But one of the notable advantages of the new closures now proliferating is that if your wine comes with a polymer 'cork' or a screwcap, you can safely store it upright.

Wine and food

Wine is made to be drunk with food, but some wines go better with particular dishes than others. It is no coincidence that Italian wines, characterised by soft, cherry fruit and a clean, mouth-drying finish, go so well with the sticky delights of pasta.

But it's personal taste rather than national associations that should determine the choice of wine with food. And if you prefer a black-hearted Argentinian Malbec to a brambly Italian Barbera with your Bolognese, that's fine.

The conventions that have grown up around wine and food pairings do make some sense, just the same. I was thrilled to learn in the early days of my drinking career that sweet, dessert wines can go well with strong blue cheese. As I don't much like puddings, but love sweet wines, I was eager to test this match – and I'm here to tell you that it works very well indeed as the end-piece to a grand meal in which there is cheese as well as pud on offer.

Red wine and cheese are supposed to be a natural match, but I'm not so sure. Reds can taste awfully tinny with soft cheeses such as Brie and Camembert, and even worse with goat's cheese. A really extravagant, yellow Australian Chardonnay will make a better match. Hard cheeses such as Cheddar and the wonderful Old Amsterdam (top-of-the-market Gouda) are better with reds.

And then there's the delicate issue of fish. Red wine is supposed to be a no-no. This might well be true of grilled and wholly unadorned white fish, such as sole or a delicate dish of prawns, scallops or crab. But what about oven-roasted monkfish or a substantial winter-season fish pie? An edgy red will do very well indeed, and provide much comfort for those many among us who simply prefer to drink red wine with food, and white wine on its own.

It is very often the method by which dishes are prepared, rather than their core ingredients, that determines which wine will work best. To be didactic, I would always choose Beaujolais or summer-fruit-style reds such as those from Pinot Noir grapes to go with a simple roast chicken. But if the bird is cooked as coq au vin with a hefty wine sauce, I would plump for a much more assertive red.

Some sauces, it is alleged, will overwhelm all wines. Salsa and curry come to mind. I have carried out a number of experiments into this great issue of our time, in my capacity as consultant to a company that specialises in supplying wines to Asian restaurants. One discovery I have made is that forcefully fruity dry white wines with keen acidity can go very well indeed even with fairly incendiary dishes. Sauvignon Blanc with Madras? Give it a try!

I'm also convinced, however, that some red wines will stand up very well to a bit of heat. The marvellously robust reds of Argentina made from Malbec grapes are good partners to Mexican chilli-hot recipes and salsa dishes. The dry, tannic edge to these wines provides a good counterpoint to the inflammatory spices in the food.

Some foods are supposedly impossible to match with wine. Eggs and chocolate are among the prime offenders. And yet, legendary cook Elizabeth David's best-selling autobiography was entitled *An Omelette and a Glass of Wine,* and the affiliation between chocolates and champagne is an unbreakable one. Taste is, after all, that most personally governed of all senses. If your choice is a boiled egg washed down with a glass of claret, who is to dictate otherwise?

Index